# AA

# SHORT WALKS
## – to –
# COUNTRY PUBS

Produced by the Publishing Division of the Automobile Association
Cover design by Design Directions Ltd
Illustrations by Alan Roe and Pamela Hankey

Edited by David Hancock

Additional research by F and S.C. Dunford, Derek Emmott,
T and F Fagan, Dominic Goldberg, Derek and Evelyn Hancock,
Shiona Hardie, Daniel Holder, Giala Murray, Janice Murray,
R.C.J. Rhodes, Bert Tasker, Alec Taylor

Printed and bound by BPCC Wheatons Ltd, Exeter

Every effort is made to ensure accuracy, but the publishers do not hold
themselves responsible for any consequences that may arise from errors
or omissions. Whilst the contents are believed correct at the time of
going to press, changes may have occurred since that time or will occur
during the currency of this book

First published, April 1991
Second edition, June 1992
Third edition © The Automobile Association, May 1993

A CIP catalogue record for this book is available from the British Library

Published by The Automobile Association, Fanum House, Basingstoke,
Hampshire RG21 2EA

ISBN 0 7495 0730 6

# Contents

# Introduction

## ~Using the guide~

If you have been using either the first or second edition of Short Walks to Country Pubs, you will be pleased to know that, as for the second edition, about 20 per cent of the walks and pubs in this third edition are new to the guide. Every walk, whether it is included for the first time or has been there since the first edition, has been checked and updated.

We have made every effort to ensure that the descriptions of the walks and the pubs are correct, nevertheless we accept no liability for errors or omissions or for any consequences arising from them. Despite our best efforts to ensure accuracy, changes may occur at any stage during the lifetime of the book.

## ~The pubs~

Each pub (bar one which is the startpoint) forms the midpoint of a walk and has a short description intended to convey its character, the sort of food you may find, the hours when bar food is served, and the beers and ciders on draught. All these details may change at short notice and, although the licensees have supplied us with the information in good faith, it should be taken as a guide only.

## ~The walks~

The walks, mostly round trips, have all been carefully chosen to take you through attractive and varied areas of the English countryside, to be enjoyable both for experienced and occasional walkers, and to have an average total length of around six miles. The approximate distance is always stated, but the time it will take to do the walk will vary considerably with the individual. Generally speaking, it is safe to think in terms of an average speed of two miles an hour.

At the beginning of each walk, we give an indication of the conditions you should expect, for example, whether it is a gentle stroll on reasonably level ground, or a more challenging walk on rougher terrain with hills to climb. If a walk includes any particularly steep hill stretches, or if paths tend to get very muddy in wet weather, we have said so.

## ~Directions and maps~

Route directions for the walks are as detailed as we can make them, but we believe it is essential to take a large-scale walkers' map with you - the Ordnance Survey 1: 50 000 Landranger series, for example, is ideal. The paths and tracks used are all marked on these maps, and, if you should have the misfortune to miss your way, or need to make a detour for any reason, you will need such a map to reorientate yourself. The sheet number of the appropriate OS 1: 50 000 map for every walk is given under the heading 'Parking' in the first column.

## ~ Parking ~

Places are suggested where you may be able to park. These have all been checked by our researchers and were found to be practicable - some are in fact official car parks. However, these suggestions are not a guarantee of any right to leave a vehicle parked. Please remember that it is the responsibility of the individual to ensure that his or her vehicle is safely and not illegally parked and that it does not obstruct other traffic or access.

## ~ Clothing ~

Do wear sensible clothes, and remember that in this country the weather is notoriously changeable, so it is sensible to take a waterproof. You also need comfortable footwear that will withstand wet and possibly muddy or slippery conditions. Light walking boots or well-fitting wellingtons with a good sole are recommended.

## Public footpaths, ~ rights of way, ~ country code

Our routes follow public rights of way and established paths, tracks and bridleways wherever possible, but the routes sometimes include stretches along a road. Even small country lanes can be deceptive, so keep children and dogs close to you at all times, and walk so that you can see any approaching traffic in good time.

Keep dogs on a lead if there are farm animals about - your pet may be reliable and not apt to chase or bite - but farm animals, especially cows with young calves, can take violent exception to dogs they do not know.

When using a public footpath or right of way, you should not encounter any animals more alarming than cattle or sheep. In some circumstances, however, landowners have the right to put a bull in a field crossed by a public footpath. It is often said that a bull with a herd of cows is no threat, but as a general rule it is best to assume that bulls are completely unpredictable and take no chances.

Do keep to the designated paths, and if you come to a field with crops, walk round the edge, not across the middle. If you open a gate, please remember to close it after you. Be particularly careful not to discard cans, bags, bottles or food because these are a hazard to farm animals as well as being an eyesore. If you do find that a public right of way has been blocked, for whatever reason, it is better to inform the Rights of Way Officer in the Highways and Traffic Department of the County Council than to attempt to argue or force a way through.

# Weston to Branscombe

∽ Approximately 6 miles ∽

*Coastal walk along part of the East Devon footpath affording fine views of Beer Head, Portland Bill and Torbay. The scrub-covered hillside accommodates badgers, and the undisturbed undergrowth of the coast slips is perfect for finches and warblers. Buzzards and kestrels can also be seen.*

**Parking**

OS Map Ref SY1688 Leave your car at the NT car park at Weston.

**Further Exploration**

Branscombe is a scattered village of pretty, stone, thatched cottages nestling in three deep combes. There you will find an old forge, built of wood and still working.

St. Winifred's Church was built in the 12th century, and there still remain fragments of a medieval wall-painting, probably representing Belshazzar's Feast.

Follow the NT signs southwest to Weston Combe and at a fork, bear left to follow the coast path for nearly two miles. Soon after passing the fort remains on your left, you will come to a junction of footpaths. Take the right-hand path signposted to Branscombe Mouth. Drop downhill beside the Lookout Hotel towards the car park, turn left by the stream and follow the path across the meadows to Branscombe and turn left to the pub.

## Mason's Arms (Free House)

This is a popular, creeper-clad, 14th-century inn with a pretty terrace and colourful gardens which have ample seating. Inside the low-beamed, rambling pub, there is a massive central hearth - spit roasts are cooked here during winter on Thursday lunchtimes - around which chairs, cushioned wall benches and settles, are arranged on the flagstones. Children are not allowed in the bar.

On draught: Bass, Worthington, Fergusons Dartmoor, Wadworth 6X, Guinness, Lowenbrau, Carlsberg, Autumn cider, Luscombes cider. Food: there is a wide range at lunchtime, from ploughman's lunches (£3), to steamed steak and kidney pudding (£5.25), and locally caught fish; times are 12-2pm and 7-9pm. There is a separate restaurant.

Telephone: 029780 300 or 304.

Turn right out of the inn, towards Upper Branscombe and walk along the lane until you reach St Winifred's Church. Take the footpath through the churchyard, which will bring you out in the woods above the combe. Turn right and climb up towards Berry Barton, making sure to keep right when the path forks. At Berry Barton, follow the quiet lane west for about a mile back to Weston.

# Start Point to East Prawle

~ Approximately 6½ miles ~

Leave the car park through a gate and follow a path towards Great Mattiscombe Sand, down to the coast. Join the main coastal footpath and follow this to Lannacombe Beach. Remain on the coastal path back to Start Point and on towards Prawle Point - the extreme southern tip of Devon. The word 'Prawle' comes from an old English word meaning 'look-out hill'. The rocky path soon levels onto grassland near Maelcombe House. Towards the end of the grassland above the long shingle beach, follow a sign pointing to East Prawle, to a gate and shortly bear right up a steep grassy hill, and over a wall. Turn right onto a path and join the road into the village to reach the pub.

*Coastal walk passing a number of coves and beaches, with a contrasting return walk across undulating farmland with views inland of typical rolling Devon hills. Wildlife is abundant: look out for finches, pipits, cormorants, gulls and colourful aromatic flowers and shrubs.*

## Pig's Nose (Free House)

Located close to a small green at the centre of this hilltop village, this unpretentious white-walled pub follows an unusual theme inside, with pig posters and a cabinet of pig ornaments. Children are welcome.

On draught: Flowers IPA, Boddingtons, Wadworth 6X, Murphy's, Heineken, Stella Artois. Food: the menu offers honey-roast ham (£3.75), plaice and chips (£3.95) and ploughmans from £2.60. Of particular note are the sandwiches, including fresh crab (£3.25), prawn (£2.25) and cheese (£1.40). Specialities include home-made lasagne (£3.90) and treacle tart with clotted cream; times are 12-2pm and 6-9.30pm.

Telephone: 054851 209.

From the pub, bear left along the road to a T-junction, turn right, and right again at a phone box. Follow the lane, ignoring the turning to Maelcombe House. Paths are waymarked with blue arrows on posts, through two farms - Woodcombe and Higher Borough and across fields. Remain on the path down a steep combe to a road, bear right and follow signposts back to Start Point.

**Parking**

OS Map 202 Ref SX8237 Start Point car park (charge and supervised during the summer, free in winter).

**Further Exploration**

A short diversion can be made to Start Point lighthouse where fine views can be had across to Slapton Sands and Dartmouth. The lighthouse directs those vessels sailing in-shore, to avoid the Skerries, a dangerous bank off the coast.

# Cox Tor to Peter Tavy

∽ Approximately 5 miles ∽

*This scenic walk encompasses open rugged moorland and the undulating landscape of the Tavy valley with panoramic views into Cornwall and of the surrounding tors. There is a steep climb on the return journey.*

**Parking**

OS Map 191 SX 5375. Viewpoint car park on the B3357, 3 miles east of Tavistock.

**Further Exploration**
Merrivale Stone Rows
Located on the moor east of Tavistock, the stones are one of Dartmoor's most interesting prehistoric remains and include a circle, cairns and standing stones.

Brent Tor
North of Peter Tavy this cone of volcanic rock rising 1,100 ft above sea level is topped by the small, mostly 13th-century, church of St Michael.

From the viewpoint monument head north across the road onto the moor for approximately 200 yards, then remain at the same contour level and start to circle round Cox Tor (towering above you on the right) in a clockwise direction looking out for a grassy swath. Shortly, cross a stream and follow the swath through stands of bracken to reach a lane. Cross over and head down towards the distant stone wall, skirting round slightly to the right to pass within a few hundred yards of a farmhouse. Keep the wall to your left, following it to a tall stile, then take the path across two fields (wall on left) towards a small farm. Pass through a gate, then walk alongside the farmhouse to another high stile, beyond which head diagonally down the field and out onto a lane. Turn left, then right at the T-junction and pass Harragrove Farm. Beyond a left-hand bend take the footpath to the right, then make for the church tower across several fields and banks,via awkward stone steps and rejoin the lane down into the village of Peter Tavy. Turn right at the Post Office and cross the Collybrook for the church and pub.

## Peter Tavy Inn (Free House)

Located near the church, this thick-walled 15th-century inn is full of charm, especially in the small heavily beamed main bar which has a flagstone floor, a large woodburner set in a huge stone fireplace and sturdy settles and wooden tables. Beyond the food servery is the restaurant.

On draught: Wadworth 6X, Fremlins Bitter, Tetley Bitter, Wethered Winter Royal, Guinness, Skol, Carlsberg Export, Inch's Stonehouse cider. Food: blackboard menu features interesting dishes including nut roast (£1.50), crepe stuffed with spinach and garlic (£3), game pie (£2.10), mixed salads (£2.50-£3.50), soup and Sunday roast (£4.75), honey and oat flan and fruit pies and crumbles (£1.25); times are 12-2.15pm and 7-9.30pm. The restaurant, specialises in fish.

Telephone 0822 810348.

Retrace your steps back to the Post Office, turn left onto a track and walk parallel with the river. On reaching a road turn left, cross the river and proceed uphill to where the road becomes a footpath beyond Combe Cottages. Keep on through a gate to a crossroads of tracks, take the path marked 'The Moor via The Combe' and cross the footbridge, then pass under electric wires before following the boulder-strewn path up a steep hill, keeping the stone wall on the right. At the top turn right onto a walled grassy lane, then beyond a gate bear slightly left across rough ground. Pass some craggy rocks on the right and follow the stone wall (now on your left) to a lane, turn left, then immediately bear half-right onto the open moor to follow a grassy swath and climb gradually uphill in a clockwise direction. After half a mile look for the remains of hut settlements, then bear right and head for the crest of the rise, keeping the small pool to the left. Descend on the wide grassy strips back to the road and car park.

### Lydford

This village once had a royal mint and the Castle Inn possesses four silver 'Lydford Pennies'. The real castle was built as a stannary prison in 1195 and is said to be haunted by Judge Jeffries, amongst others. The nearby gorge (NT) formed by the River Lyd is spectacular with various dramatic features and the 90ft-high White Lady Waterfall. Telephone 082282 441 or 320

### Mary Tavy

Peter Tavy's sister village was once a prosperous copper-mining village and Wheal Betsy (NT), located off the A386, is the best surviving engine house on Dartmoor, once pumping Prince Arthur Consols mine which produced lead, silver and zinc.

# Becky Falls to Lustleigh

~ Approximately.5½ miles ~

*Outstanding views across beautiful countryside and into wooded river valleys, are the essence of this walk along the edge of Dartmoor. The network of trails takes you through the Bovey Valley nature reserve, the home of flycatchers, warblers, dippers and wagtails and a wealth of wild flowers.*

**Parking**

OS Map 191 Ref SK7580. Becky Falls car park - open 10am-6pm (5pm winter) £2.50 per day (free in winter).

**Further Exploration**

**Becky Falls**

Set in 60 acres of glorious natural woodlands, Becky Brook cascades through a fairy glen and crashes 70 feet over huge granite boulders.

**Lustleigh**

A charming village, containing numerous thatched cottages and a 13th-century church with an unusual rood-screen bearing the pomegranate badge of Catherine of Aragon.

Follow the path over the road signposted to Becky Falls, then turn left, cross the footbridge and take the path to Bovey Valley and Lustleigh Cleave. The falls soon become visible on the right, and signposted. Remain on the path through mixed forest with Becky Brook down to the right, over the junction and along the trail bearing left at a fork to follow the narrow path alongside a stone wall, gradually dropping down into the heavily wooded Bovey Valley. Two-thirds of the way down, bear right at a wall, towards Clam Bridge. Cross the bridge and keep to the path gently climbing up the side of the valley. At a fork, follow a path waymarked Lustleigh via Pethybridge, to a second gate on the right and onto a track and then a road along which you bear right, then first left - Pethybridge. Fork right at a telephone box and walk down into the heart of the village. The pub is tucked down behind the church, close to the cricket ground.

## The Cleave (Free House)

This is a beautiful, white-painted, 15th-century thatched inn. Its old flagstone porch is surrounded by a neat and colourful garden which offers some very peaceful shelter in summer. Inside, a welcoming lounge bar has a low ceiling, and is comfortably furnished with settles and chairs. A second bar and family room have been recently refurbished. Children are welcome in the family room.

On draught: Marston's Pedigree, Flowers Original, guest beers like Murphy's and Heineken. Food: a varied menu of home-made dishes includes soup (£1.95), steak and kidney pie (£5.45), and beef in cider (£4.95) Desserts change daily and range from chocolate mousse to treacle tart (£1.95). Service is pleasant and efficient, and portions generous; times are 12-2pm and 7-9pm (8.30pm Oct-Mar). Pub closed Mon in Jan and Feb. Cream teas are served from 3-5.30pm in summer.

Telephone: 06477 223.

L eaving the pub, pass the church and follow the road signposted to Rudge, up a steep hill. At the T-junction, take the footpath ahead waymarked to Bovey Valley, into which the well-defined path descends after skirting Hisley Farm, gradually winding down through thick woodland to an ancient packhorse bridge over the river. Pass through a gate and bear right onto an established track, signposted to Manaton. Keep on this path back over the river and shortly take a right fork up the steep valley, rejoining your outward route, and return to Becky Falls.

# Torcross to Slapton

~ Approximately 5 miles ~

*This walk offers coastal views along Slapton Sands, and a peaceful nature trail alongside the Ley with its abundant wildlife and reedbeds.*

**Parking:**

OS Map 202 Ref SX8242
Torcross Car Park.

**Further Exploration**

Torcross

Pleasant old houses line the seafront along Start Bay at Torcross. The village was once the most easterly pilchard-fishing village until the pilchard shoals disappeared from the south-west coast.

Slapton

Many houses in its twisting streets have had their walls rendered to hide shell damage suffered in World War 11 when the US army took over the village for manoeuvres. It is dominated by a great 80ft-high tower, north of the church, which is built of slate and is the remains of a College of Chantry Priests founded in 1373. The church has a 14th-century medieval spire.

Either follow the path beside Slapton Ley eastwards, between the road and Ley, or cross the road and walk along the top of the beach. Follow the beach or Ley path to a memorial and take the road signposted to Slapton on the left. Cross the bridge over the stream at the end of the Ley and enter the nature reserve through a gate on the left. Follow the nature trail to the north of the Ley to a gate. Turn left onto a duckboard path which weaves along for a short distance and then keep to the path signposted 'Deer Bridge' until you reach a quiet lane. Turn right and follow the road uphill then down into Slapton.

## Tower Inn (Free House)

An ancient 14th-century inn, this was once a row of cottages for the workers who helped to build the monastery of which only the tower remains. Inside, the air of antiquity is preserved in the three bars, with flagstone floors, low-backed settles, and small armchairs. Two bars have log fires. Children are welcome in the restaurant, side room and garden.

On draught: Hall & Woodhouse Tanglefoot, Eldridge Pope Royal Oak, Gibbs Mew Bishop's Tipple, Palmers IPA, Wadworth 6X, Murphy's, Stella Artois. Food: a good range of food includes various pastas (from £4.50) and large 9-inch pizzas with numerous toppings (around £5.50) and steaks, basket meals, shellfish and ploughman's; times are 12-2.30pm and 7-9.30pm.

Telephone: 0548 580216.

Return to the lane, bear left and follow it through the village, turning left past the Post Office and keeping to the lane back down to Slapton Ley and the beach. Turn right back along the Ley to the car park.

# Fowey to Polkerris

~ Approximately 6½ miles ~

Follow footpath signs to the town centre. At the general store, bear right and follow the road down into Readymoney Cove, and then join the coastal footpath up into Carington Wood. At the first bend, bear right and follow Love Lane, heading inland. At a quiet lane, turn left and then right at a T-junction towards a small hamlet. At Lankelly Farm, take the footpath on the left down into a combe and follow the yellow stickers across stiles, through meadows, and past two farms . At a lane beside Tregaminion church, turn right and then left through the first gate. You will soon join the coast path down through a wood to the small fishing hamlet of Polkerris.

## Rashleigh Inn (Free House)

This marvellously placed pub has picnic tables on its stone terrace overlooking an isolated beach and small jetty. Inside local photographs and prints adorn the panelled walls. There is a small restaurant area where children are welcome.

On draught: St Austell Hicks Special, Burton Ale, Furguson Bolsters Bitter, Guinness, Lowenbrau. Food: the menu includes stock pot soup (£1.75), sandwiches from £1.60, fish pie (£5), cottage pie (£4.50), and an interesting salad bar; times are 12-2pm and 7-10.30pm (Sun 7-9.45pm).

Telephone: 072681 3991.

Leaving the pub, retrace your steps back through the woods, remaining on the coastal footpath. This path is a fine undulating cliff walk, crossing National Trust land, namely Gribbin Head and its 84ft beacon built in 1832 to help vessels navigate safely around the headland. From Gribbin head, the established path undulates down into small isolated caves and valleys. The path eventually rejoins the outward route at Love Lane to return to central Fowey.

*The outward route takes you along flower-filled paths, woodland and open meadow; the contrasting return route is a coastal walk over cliffs and down into coves with fine views across the estuary, of Polruan and of the china clay area near St Austell.*

**Parking**

OS Map 200 Ref SX1251. Main Fowey car park (£1 per day).

**Further Exploration**

Fowey is one of Cornwall's most historic and romantic places, with its narrow lanes and colourful old houses. Large tankers anchor in the deep waters of the estuary as they are loaded with china clay - Fowey remains one of Cornwall's leading exporters.

St Catherine's Castle (English Heritage) was one of the many strongholds built by Henry VIII to defend the coast. It was restored in 1855 and is open daily (free).

Polkerris was one of the busiest pilchard-fishing harbours of the last century.

# Coombe to Crosstown

∽ Approximately 6½ miles ∽

*This walk is quite strenuous and takes you along remote, wild cliffs with magnificent views of the dramatic coastline, through deep, green valleys, rolling farmland and peaceful, wooded river trails. On the coast birdlife is abundant - watch out for buzzards, ravens, jackdaws, rock pipits and gulls.*

**Parking**

OS Map 190 Ref SS2011. Duckpool car park.

**Further Exploration**

Morwenstow is Cornwall's northernmost parish, and is best known for its former vicar - the poet, Robert Stephen Hawker, who came here in 1834 and spent 40 years serving a congregation that included smugglers, wreckers and dissenters. An extraordinary man, he felt deeply for mariners wrecked on this coast and often scrambled down the high cliffs to carry their bodies up to the church for a Christian burial - each has his own grave, but no headstone.

From the car, follow the coastal path (waymarked) on your right, which wends its way round a few headlands down into steep, unspoilt combes. Don't be put off by the white dish aerials, these are soon left behind. At the second combe - Tidna Combe - follow the footpath inland, soon running beside a small stream. The path passes through varied vegetation which changes as one leaves the harsher conditions of the coast. The taller plants and shrubs begin to dominate and the valley becomes very sheltered and alive with insect and birdlife. Follow the path to the end of the valley, up some steps to the stile, across a field uphill to another stile, before entering the far corner of the pub's garden in the hamlet of Crosstown.

## The Bush (Free House)

This delightful, ancient, country pub, reputed to be one of the oldest in Britain, is very welcoming. It was once a monastic rest-house on a pilgrim route, and records date back to AD 950 when it was a hermit's cell. Of particular note is the Celtic piscina carved from serpentine stone still set in one wall. The three bars have heavy slate-flagged floors, the main bar being quite small with old built-in settles, and a huge stone fireplace, while the Snug side has antique seats, old elm trestle tables and walls decorated with miner's lamps, casks, funnels, blue plates, clocks and various prints of the pub. The small windows look out across the fields to the sea. No children under 14 are allowed in the bars but there is some seating outside in the sunken courtyard.

On draught: St Austell Hicks Special and Tinners Ale, Worthington Best, Bass, Inch's Cider. Food: The short lunchtime menu offers good value for money - soup (£1.20), beef stew and roll (£2.25), ploughmans (£1.75), pasty (£1.20) and sandwiches (£1.20). Food is served at 12-2pm. Closed Mon from Oct to Mar.

Telephone: 028883 242.

Retrace your route back down into Tidna Combe as far as the river. Cross over the bridge and the stile, and follow the edge of the field to another stile and on to a track. To the left is Tonacombe, a 15th-century Tudor manor house. Pass through a gate into arable fields. When the crop is high, walk along the edge of two fields, crossing the stiles before reaching a lane and Stanbury Farm. Walk up the driveway to the farm, keeping the house to your right and the pond to your left, to a gate. Follow the yellow arrows across two fields to join a lane at Eastaway Manor. Cross the lane and pass through a gate, keeping to the path beside the Manor. Cross a stile and continue, following the arrows, across the fields to the hamlet of Woodford, emerging on a lane opposite the chapel. Bear right, then right again at a thatched cottage, and follow the lane past a farm before joining the waymarked path to the right. Remain on this across the fields and through a gate down into the valley, making sure when entering woodland to take the track which runs at right angles to that which you are following, down to a small stream. Follow the yellow arrows on posts across the stream, then bear right and follow the beautiful wooded valley down towards Coombe valley. At the road, bear right down into the hamlet of Coombe. Keep on the quiet lane and follow the sign to Duckpool back to the beach.

The church of St Morwenna is superbly situated, almost in a dell between the towering cliffs and its tower has always been a landmark for passing ships. The doorway is carved with heads of men and beasts, and inside are some fine Norman arches and carved bench ends. Next to the church, the rectory shows Robert Hawker's eccentricity in the unusual chimneys - modelled on the towers of churches he had known, and one modelled on his mother's tomb. A few hundred yards south along the coast path is the driftwood hut where he wrote much of his poetry.

# St Anthony-in-Meneage to Helford

〜 Approximately 4¼ miles 〜

*A beautiful wooded shoreline and estuary walk through a very tranquil landscape . Birds likely to be seen include cormorants, many herons, shelduck, curlews and kingfishers.*

**Parking**

OS Map 204 SW7825
In summer, car park close to parish church, or anywhere near the church.

**Further Exploration**

The area incorporating Helford, Manaccan and St Anthony, forms the Lizard Peninsula known as Meneage - 'Monkish land'. Celtic monks brought Christianity to the district, and formed hermitages and settlements, out of which arose the earliest churches of Cornwall.

**St Antony-in-Meneage**

The beautiful church was reputedly built by a band of shipwrecked Normans to thank St Anthony' for saving their lives. Some credibility is given to this tale by the fact that the town is built of a granite found only in Normandy. The church is lit by candlelight - brass candle holders hang from the ceiling - and a candlelit evensong is held.

Leave the car park, turning left onto a quiet lane, passing the church and a small boat park on the edge of the creek. Keep to the lane until the second corner, where you pass through a gate on the right to join the coastal footpath, bearing left. Keep to the coastal path through the heavily wooded slopes of the Helford river, down into small coves and beaches. It is important to keep strictly to the footpath through the wooded areas from St Antony because the land is owned by the Bosahan estate. No dogs are allowed on this stretch. When the footpath meets a quiet lane, bear right and then left onto the coast path just past a house called the 'Old Pilchard Shed'. Follow this path to Helford. Cross the footbridge over the creek and follow the lane to the pub.

Return across the footbridge, bear right and follow the footpath, signposted to Manaccan, to a heavily wooded valley with a small stream and active birdlife. The path gradually winds up out of the woods and crosses a meadow, road and a second field into the small village of Manaccan. Reaching a second road, cross by the antique shop and follow the lane down to the church. From there, follow the bridleway (waymarked) opposite the church gate and remain on this until you reach a lane at the creek side. Turn left and follow the lane along Gillan Creek for the return to the car park.

# Shipwright's Arms (Whitbread)

This fine thatched pub has a terrace dropping down to the water's edge, offering a peaceful, secluded view of this lovely wooded creek. Benches sit amongst palm trees and flowers, and the pub entrance is decorated by colourful hanging baskets. Inside, there are comfortable oak settles and an open fire. A nautical theme is created by collections of model ships, sea pictures, navigational lamps, and drawings of people in the pub or village in years past. Children are welcome in the eating area or on the terrace.

On draught: Flowers IPA, Castle Eden Ale, Guinness, Heineken, Strongbow. Food: there is a wide range of meat, fish, cheese, and pasties, and a good salad bar, with prices averaging from £4-£6. Evening meals include steaks and Mexican chicken, and prices start at £6.25; times are 12-2pm and 7-9pm, but there is no bar food on Sun and Mon evenings in winter.

Telephone: 032623 235.

A short diversion can be made along the coastal path to 'Dennis Head' (from the Cornish word 'dinas', meaning castle), once an Iron-Age cliff castle.

### Helford

This snug village with small, white-washed, thatched cottages tucked away by the creek, once had a bad reputation as a smugglers' haunt, and there are still cellars which are reputed to have been their secret stores. Frenchman's Creek, made famous by Daphne du Maurier's novel of that name, lies a short distance to the west of Helford.

### Manaccan

Believed to date from AD 967, this small village has cottages clustering round its ancient church, which has a fig tree growing out of the south-west wall reputed to have been there for 200 years.

# Porthgwarra to Treen

∾ Approximately 4½ miles ∾

*This is a rugged coastline walk, with dramatic headlands contrasting with sheltered sandy beaches, followed by a quiet farmland return route.*

**Parking**

OS Map 203 Ref SW3621. Porthgwarra car park. (50p)

**Further Exploration**

The Minack Theatre is an incredible Greek-style amphitheatre hewn out of the cliffside 70 metres above the sea and offers audiences a spectacular natural backdrop. Productions are staged during the summer months in the evenings, and the theatre can be viewed (entrance charge) during the day.

Porthcurno beach is a broad stretch of white sand in a cove sheltered by jagged arms of granite. It was here that the first transatlantic cable was brought ashore. Take care on the steep path down to it.

Logan Rock weighs over 65 tons, and can be rocked. In 1824, 12 sailors dislodged it, but the Admiralty insisted that they replace it.

B ear left past the small shop, keeping the beach to your right. Follow the waymarked coastal path uphill past a house before heading right along the cliff top. Remain on the coastal path to the isolated and spectacular cove of Porth Chapel with its sandy beach. The path passes St Leven Holy Well (whose water is still used for baptisms) and ancient stone steps lead down to the beach and the site of a ruined chapel. Follow the footpath up onto the headland of Pean-Men-An-Mere (where there are remains of a radio mast - Cable and Wireless Company's attempt to monitor Marconi's experiment) and onto Porthcurno, where the path passes the Minack Theatre. Keep to the coastal path to a National Trust sign, then take the path on the left inland over fields to Treen.

## Logan Rock (St Austell)

This old and unspoilt inn has great charm and character with a low-beamed, rambling bar containing high-backed modern oak settles, wall seats and tables, and a large fireplace. There is also a snug, and a family bar at the rear where food can be ordered. A small attractive garden with tables looks out over open fields and there are also picnic tables in the front courtyard. Children are welcome in the garden and the family room, and dogs are allowed in on a lead. Make a point of looking at the different pictures on either side of the inn sign.

On draught: Tinners Ale, Hicks Special, Bosuns, Guinness, Carlsberg. Food: a good choice of basic bar food is served in generous portions. The menu includes homemade lentil soup (£1.50), sandwiches (from £1.10), lasagne and salad (£3.50), baked potatoes and fillings from (£2.25) and steak meals (from £6.50); times are 12-2pm, 7-9pm. Open all day Jul-Sep. Baby foods can be heated on request.

Telephone: 0736 810495.

**R**eturn back up the lane past the tea rooms and, at the corner, bear right, heading towards the thatched cottage. Turn right in front of the cottage, and then follow the path across six fields and into Trendrennan Farm. Go through the farmyard, following the footpath sign, and head towards three masts ahead, crossing three fields and gates. Pass close to the post holding mast wire, cross a stile and bear right down the slope onto a track and along to the lane. Cross the road onto another track, through a gate, and across a field to Rospletha Farm. Through the gate, follow the clear path across two fields towards St Levan's Church, and enter the churchyard over the stile. Reaching the road, bear left and, in a short distance, take the footpath on your right and bear right again at a junction, following the path which soon rejoins the outward route back along the coastal path to Porthgwarra.

# Wells to Croscombe

∽ Approximately 5 miles ∽

*A fairly level walk across pasture and farmland through the Sheppey Valley. One steep hill on the return journey and open views across Sedgemoor to Glastonbury Tor.*

**Parking**
OS Map 182 Ref ST 5546
Public car parks in Wells

**Further Exploration**
Wells
England's smallest city gained its name from the fresh springs of water that bubble up in the bottom of the Bishop's garden. The west front of the Cathedral has 356 statues set in ornate niches. A medieval clock graces the northern transept, performing every quarter of an hour with jousting knights on horseback and a little seated figure known as Jack Blandiver.

Wookey Hole
Where the River Axe emerges from beneath the Mendip Hills there is an awe-inspiring world of underground caverns and lakes, now paved and dramatically lit. Archaeologists have found evidence of the human occupation of the caves from 250BC to AD400.

From the Cathedral head for the Bishop's Palace and follow the path round the moat to the A37. Cross the road onto a rough track and shortly turn right (yellow arrow) to climb the steps up Tor Hill (NT). Once on top, keep right of a clump of brambles, pass through a copse to a stile, then follow the right-hand fence around a hidden quarry before bearing left towards a house. Cross a track and bear half-right downhill across a field towards the main road. Soon turn left along an established path to a wooden gate, keep to the right-hand edge of the following field to a green lane. Cross over, then keep right of a lone tree (yellow arrow) to a swing gate in the hedge. Beyond, follow the route across four fields towards Dinder church and join the lane into the village. Pass the church lych-gate, bear left beyond a post-box, soon to take a waymarked path on the right and cross three fields to a lane. Cross, and pass behind Higher Farm to follow a defined path over three fields and stiles to Croscombe. Turn left along the lane, and right at the end to pass the church before reaching the pub.

## Bull Terrier (Free House)

One of Somerset's oldest pubs, originally a priory, first licensed in 1612 and known as the Rose and Crown until 1976 since when it has become a popular meeting place for owners and breeders of Bull Terriers. Its three bars have loads of character, with beams, flagstones and good comfortable furnishings. There is a family room and a garden.

On draught: Smiles Best Bitter, Eldridge Pope Royal Oak, Bull Terrier, Palmers IPA, Wilkins cider. Food: reliable bar food includes home-made soup (£1.85), steak and kidney pie (£4.95), Barnsley chop (£5.95), mixed vegetable curry (£4.90), Indian spiced beans (£4.65) and chicken curry (£5.50); times are 12-2pm and 7-9.30pm (10pm Fri and Sat; Sun 12-1.45pm and 7-9pm). Nov-Mar, closed Mon.

Telephone (0749) 343648

etrace your steps back past the church and left along the lane, then almost immediately, cross the stone stile on the right and climb steeply uphill to another stile. Keep on with the yellow arrow to cross a stile and turn left along a hedged path, shortly to pass through a small gate. A defined path crosses three fields before joining a track to the left of a barn. Cross a lane and a field, pass through some scrub then bear left onto a track to a metal gate. An established path winds through pasture to a wooden gate, beyond which turn left along a metalled track to another gate where a blue arrow and post (Wells 2 miles) waymarks the route along the right-hand edge of the field. Follow blue arrow, bearing left onto a trackway which skirts King's Castle Wood Reserve and passes through Wells golf course. Pass a house on the right and cross a metal stile to follow the outward route, back over Tor Hill, to the Bishop's Palace.

# Kennisham Hill to Luxborough

*Approximately 5 miles*

*Quiet walk through the woods and valleys of the Brendon Hills, with panoramic views across neighbouring hills towards Watchet and the Welsh coast. Pheasants and buzzards can often be seen in this area.*

**Parking**

OS Map 181 Ref SS9635. Picnic area beside B3224

**Further Exploration**

Combe Sydenham Country Park, Monksilver

A few miles east of Luxborough is a 16th-century house that was once the home of Sir Francis Drake's second wife, Elizabeth. There is an Elizabethan-style garden with woodland walks, a corn mill and a children's play area. Fly fishing is also available

From the picnic area, follow the path on the left, waymarked to Wheddon Cross and Luxborough. Walk along a forest track until, approaching a farm, you follow the path through a gateway and bear right, keeping to the edge of the woodland, continuing through fields and gates. At a junction of paths, head downhill towards Luxborough, keeping to the hedge when you enter the field, until you pass through a gate at the base of a steep hill, and bear right onto a track towards the river and a farm. Before you reach the stream, turn right through a gateway and cross two fields parallel to river to reach a quiet lane and small bridge. Turn right uphill, then take the footpath arrowed to your left. Follow the path beside a stream through woodland. Cross a small footbridge, bear right to a stile, and follow the path to a lane leading to the pub.

Turn left out of the pub, right at a telephone box, and follow the lane out of the village. Cross a small bridge and turn right, following a path uphill, soon turning left onto a track waymarked Wheddon Cross via Colley Hill. Pass a pond and a cottage, then turn right at a signpost, bear right to follow a path and pass through a gateway. On nearing a house tucked down in the valley, bear right, following red markers on posts, through a gate and along the edge of a wood. Pass through another gate into the wood, follow the red markers, presently bearing right off the main track, up past a pheasant enclosure. Keep following the red markers through a gate and across a field, crossing a brook before going uphill through woodland. Pass through another gate and cross a field downhill, to a gate onto a forest track. After a short distance, take the waymarked path on the right uphill through a clearing, bear left at the top, and then follow the forest track back to the picnic area.

# Royal Oak (Free House)

This is a pub of great charm and antiquity within Exmoor National Park, located deep within a valley in the Brendon Hills. Known locally as the 'Blazing Stump', it dates back to the 15th century and remains totally unspoilt, and very welcoming, with flagstone and cobbled floors, inglenook fireplaces, and beamed ceilings. There are three bars, one of which has a massive open fire. There is a charming garden.

On draught: Batemans XXXB, Flowers IPA, Exmoor Gold, Cotleigh Tawny, guest beers, Carlsberg, Konig and Beamish. Food: good-value bar snacks include soup (£1.75), beef and Beamish pie (£4.45), lamb curry (£4.45), vegetable and stilton pie (£4.25), and ploughman's (from £3.25). Puddings include apple pie and blackberry and apple pie with custard or cream(£1.85). Traditional Sunday lunch and a separate evening menu are available; times are 12-2pm and 7-10pm (Sun 9.30pm).

Telephone: 0984 40319.

# Crewkerne to Haselbury Plucknett

## ∽ Approximately 4½ miles ∽

*An easy walk through meadows, parkland, orchards and along the banks of the River Parrett with views of the hills bordering Dorset and Somerset.*

**Parking**
OS Map 193 Ref ST4508
Crewkerne Station

**Further Exploration**
Cricket St Thomas Wildlife Park
The old and beautiful park of Cricket House has become a home for a wide variety of animals and birds including elephants, camels, llamas parrots and other exotic creatures. There are gardens, miniature railway, craft centre and restaurants. The house was used for the BBC television series 'To The Manor Born'. Telephone: 0460 30755

From the station car park walk along the A356 footway towards Crewkerne, then immediately beyond the Queens Hotel turn right onto a footpath leading into a meadow. Disregard the path that crosses diagonally, and keep close to the left-hand hedge, pass through a gap and follow the line of the hedge downhill to a stony track. Follow this to Mill Farm ahead, bearing right between the farm buildings to emerge in front of the farmhouse. Turn sharp left and follow the waymarked path through three fields to a gate and enter parkland. Keep parallel to the left-hand wire fence and make for a 'squeeze' on the left side of a coppice, then shortly cross the River Parrett. Bear right up the bank and skirt round the lower end of the big field to cross the stile visible on the far side (ignore stile on right), then climb up the steep incline to St Martin's Church. Turn left along a tarmac drive, cross a cattle grid then a stile on the right and head for the gate in the lowest corner of the field. Cross the lane and take the wide path signposted 'Haselbury Plucknett'. Beyond a stile ignore the well-worn path ahead, and bear slightly right to a stile in the hedge opposite. On reaching the village street turn right, then left just after the Old Post House to follow a narrow footpath. At the church bear round to the right to the main road; the pub lies to the left.

# Haselbury Inn (Free House)

This white-painted homely village inn has a warm and welcoming atmosphere; the 'country bar' is traditional in decor and has log fires, a relaxing area furnished with sofas and armchairs and, beyond an open beamed partition, sturdy dining tables. There is also a restaurant and a garden. Children are welcome.

On draught: Cotleigh Tawny, Butcombe Bitter, Wadworth 6X, Smiles Best, and 'guest beers' like Murphy's, Carlsberg and Warsteiner. Food: an extensive menu ranges from soup (£1.50), lasagne (£4.50), chicken and vegetable curry (£3.95), and mussels Provençale to steaks (from £9) and a choice of pizzas. Puddings may include chocolate fudge cake (£2) and apfel strudel (£2.50); times are 12-2pm, 7-10pm. Closed Mon.

Telephone: 0460 72488

Retrace your steps back to the church and follow the stony road towards Manor Farm. Turn left at crossroads of tracks, then at the main road turn right along the pavement. After 200 yards (by Chapel car park), cross the road and take the footpath which leads behind the houses to an estate road. Where this road bears right, cross the stile on the left, then immediately turn right keeping close to the hedge. On entering an orchard follow the line of tall birch trees through its centre, turning left at the end, shortly to take the next track right and proceed downhill. Where this track bears right carry on across a rough grassy patch to a stile in the fence. Beyond the stile turn left and gradually descend via terraced sheepwalks towards the river bank. Pass through a gate by some old ruins and follow the river's edge to two wooden footbridges (just after cart bridge), and cross the River Parrett and its tributary. Turn right and follow the tributary until reaching a stile, beyond which turn left and maintain course across three fields. Once over the tall stile rejoin the outward route back to Crewkerne Station

### Forde Abbey

This 12th-century Cistercian monastery was converted into a private dwelling in the mid-17th century by Cromwell's attorney general. Fine interior and 30 acres of gardens, including a kitchen garden. Telephone: 0460 20231.

### Parnham House

Fine Tudor mansion, famous as the home of John Makepeace and his furniture-making workshop. 14 acres of restored gardens, formal terraces and woodlands. Various arts events. Telephone: 0308 862204.

# Chew Magna to Stanton Wick

∽ Approximately 6 miles ∽

*A fairly flat walk through villages and open landscapes of the Chew Valley.*

### Parking

OS Map 172 Ref ST5763
Public car park behind Pelican Inn just off B3130

### Further Exploration

St Andrew's Church, Chew Magna

The building is essentially mediaeval and stands adjacent to Chew Court formerly the palace of the Bishop of Bath and Wells.. Perhaps the church's star attraction is a wooden effigy, of a knight, who smiles gently and inscrutably in the face of the problems of dating which historians have been unable to solve

Leave the car park at the barrier. Turn left, then right, following the road out of the village. Take Denny Lane to the right, turn left up a footpath and continue straight ahead passing just right of farm buildings and two houses; keep right to work around the back of Knowle Hill. Turn left along a lane, then right at T-junction, soon to pass the houses of New Town, then through a gate to the left. Cross the stream at the bottom of the field and head uphill, passing just left of a farm. Cross another lane, go through a clump of trees and head half-left for some houses. Rather than continuing past them, turn right up Moorledge Lane. After Bromley Farm go through the next gate on the left down to the far right corner of the field, over the fence and round the banks of a slate mine. Go over a plank bridge to the left, round the corner of the field, back over the dyke and a stile on the right, then uphill and to the right, over three stiles and past a derelict cottage to the left. Reaching the road, turn left and follow it round to the pub ahead.

# Carpenter's Arms (Free House)

Converted from a row of 17th-century miners' cottages, the inn looks austere from outside, with its weathered, grey, stony face; inside it is warm and lively with low oak beams, heavy curtains and open fireplaces. Though in summer patrons can choose to sit on the benches by the quiet country lane outside, the bar areas themselves get very squashed at a busy lunchtime since much of the inn is given up to serving food. Children of all ages are welcome and well-behaved dogs will be allowed on the premises.

On draught: Wadworth 6X, Bass, Butcombe, Toby, Worthington, Guinness, Murphy's, Carling, Tennent's, Stella, Dry Blackthorn cider. Food: there is a 60-seat restaurant but you can also order bar food from the Cooper's Parlour, such as sandwiches (from £2.50), ploughman's (£3.25), chicken and bacon pie (£5.95), lemon sole (£7.25) and sirloin steak (£8.95). Puddings (£2.25) may include trifle, cheesecake and rhubarb crumble; times are 12-2pm and 7-10pm; restaurant is closed Sat lunch and Sun evening.

Telephone: 0761 490202.

**Cheddar Gorge and Caves**
A few minutes away by car, visitors can explore the mysterious, deep-running caves with their glittering stactites and stalagmites, rare plants and wildlife, frozen cascades and rivers of rock.
Telephone: 0934 742343

Turn back towards the phone box, then right down Stanton Drew Lane. After about quarter of a mile, where it bends sharply to the left, leave the road and walk across the fields towards some houses. Cross the stream and a stile, and proceed over the hill to a stile in the left-hand corner, then bear right across a brook to a stile and lane. Turn left, then left again past some parking spaces, then cross Pensford Lane to go up a footpath on the right. After two stiles bear left, then half-right across a field to follow a hard track towards Stanton Drew. At the main village road, go across into Sandy Lane. Follow the track to a 'Slow, Children' sign and bear left across a stone footbridge, then head uphill to a stile, keep left to a gate and cross the river bridge before reaching the B3130. Cross the road then walk up the lime-tree avenue to Chew Court, round the house, through the churchyard, and into the village centre

# Kingston to Worth Matravers

~ Approximately 5½ miles ~

*A peaceful ramble through Purbeck downland and villages, with coastal and country views*

**Parking**

OS Map 195 Ref SY9579 Car park at Kingston village

**Further Exploration**

Kingston

This is a trim-looking estate village with a gigantic church built of Purbeck stone. Its huge tower is a notable landmark.

Worth Matravers

A quiet, unspoiled village with steep streets and stone cottages, was once an important centre for quarrying Purbeck stone which was used to build many of the churches and cathedrals across England.

Take the footpath by the noticeboard then turn right onto a lane waymarked to Hounstout. Descend the lane and bear left onto a track (to Hounstout). Cross a stile and continue along a high grassy ridge to a stile near the cliff edge. Join the coastal footpath and follow the signs towards Chapman's Pool. Remain on the path, following directional stone tablets around the steep-sided valley, and take the waymarked path towards Renscomb on the left. Cross two fields, heading towards a small car park on the left, cross a stile in the wall, over the track and another stile, and follow the footpath signposted to Worth. On reaching a farmyard track, bear left, then right onto a lane to Worth Matravers. Pass the church and a small green, before bearing left uphill to reach the pub.

Retrace your steps past the church to the children's play area. Pass through the kissing gate and follow the path waymarked to Hill Bottom along the left-hand edge of the field, over a wall stile, passing between two houses, and over a further stile into a cultivated field. Keep to the left-hand edge of the field, heading towards the quarry. Cross a stile in the far corner of the field and remain on the path that skirts around the quarry through a narrow valley, bearing right at a junction towards Afflington Barn. Eventually, you will pass through a gate and emerge from the valley and cross a field with an ancient tumulus to the right, then follow the track on the left up to a farm and a road. Cross the road and follow the waymarked bridleway downhill until you reach a footpath marker post. Bear left, following the yellow arrow up through a copse, to cross a stile and fields, and head towards a small church. At a road, turn right, then bear left at the Scott Arms pub and return to the car park.

# Square & Compass (Whitbread)

This 17th-century building is named after the tools used in stone-quarrying, an important local trade of the past. Enter the old flag-stone corridor to a small servery with two hatchways which serve good ales tapped from the cask. There are two bars, both old-fashioned; one is light and plain, with wall-benches, old tables, glass-fronted cupboards filled with old bottles, and prints and photos of old quarrymen and other characters of the past, on the walls. The larger bar is darker with different styles of tables and chairs around an old stone fireplace. Numerous paintings and photos of the pub in days past decorate the walls, along with a few decorative plates. Outside, there is a seating area which you share with several hungry chickens. Children are welcome.

On draught: Whitbread Pompey Royal and Strong Country, Marston's Pedigree, Guinness, Bulmer's Cider. Food: there are snacks such as fresh crab sandwiches, good filled rolls, and various pies and pasties; times are 12-2pm and 7-10pm. Telephone: 0929 229.

# Halstock to Corscombe

∽ Approximately 6 miles ∽

*A peaceful rural walk along established tracks affording panoramic views into Somerset towards the Mendip Hills*

**Parking**

OS Map 194 Ref ST5308

Halstock village hall

**Further Exploration**

The church at West Chelborough is worth visiting, it contains a 17th-century stone effigy tomb of a mother and child, a rhyming epitaph to Elizabeth Greenham who died in 1715, aged 28 and a 12th-century font.

**Mapperton Manor Gardens**

Located 4 miles south of Corscombe, this fine Tudor house is surrounded by several acres of terraced hillside gardens. The village that once existed nearby was wiped out by the great plague of 1660. Telephone: 0308 862645.

From the village hall, turn left and walk the short distance along the lane into the village centre. By the small green, turn right and walk south along a quiet lane passing Dogwells Farm before bearing left along a metalled road leading to Crockermoor Farm. Where the road bears left towards the farm, carry straight on along a wide bridleway (can be very muddy) and remain on this, eventually crossing a small stream and entering a large field. Proceed up the short hill and then gradually ascend the field towards the village ahead. Pass through a metal gate and make for the left-hand corner of the field to join a path (blue arrow) heading uphill towards the church, eventually into the hamlet of West Chelborough. At the telephone box, turn right and follow the track through the farmyard and buildings of Manor Farm. Through a gate into a field, keep straight ahead over the rise on an established track that bears left through a gate onto a wide grassy path. Follow this around to the right and make for the gate in the right-hand corner. Cross the field ahead keeping to the left-hand hedge, through a further gate and onto a pronounced track. At a T-junction of paths, turn right downhill to a small gate before bearing diagonally left across a field towards the house ahead. On joining the metalled lane, turn left and left again at the junction with a country lane. The pub lies a short distance along on the left.

On leaving the pub, take the lane ahead which passes over a small stream and head uphill bearing right on to another narrow lane. At a T-junction turn right and on reaching a white house ('Pines'), bear right again onto a well-established track (can be very muddy after rain). Keep straight ahead where the track bears left and remain on this wide, rutted bridleway through a small copse before passing the entrance to Halstock Golf Club. Rejoining the lane into Halstock village, bear left here and follow the lane back to the village hall.

# Fox (Free House)

The Fox is a pretty thatched pub of stone and cob built around 1640 and tucked away in a peaceful spot by a small stream. The entrance lobby is decorated with a wild flower and ivy mural and beyond are two welcoming bars, one with hunting prints and the other prettily furnished with blue gingham curtains and tablecloths and warmed by a real log fire within a huge stone fireplace. Walking boots are no problem as there are flagstone floors. Walls are adorned with copper and pewterware as well as an array of stuffed owls in glass cases. There is a family room, a garden and an outdoor play area..

On draught: Greene King Abbot Ale, Exmoor Ale, Carlsberg, Autumn Gold and Bridge Farm local cider. Food: as the board outside states, there are 'no microwaves or chips' here, just good home cooking including soup (£1.80), country pâté (£3.60), beef stew (£4.75), cauliflower cheese (£3.25) and chicken in cream sauce (£6.25).Puddings like treacle tart, bread and butter pudding and gooseberry tart are home-made and cost £2; times are 12-2pm and 7-9pm.

Telephone: 0935 891330.

# Piddletrenthide to Plush

*≈ Approximately 5 miles ≈*

*An undulating ramble across the Dorset Downs affording spectacular views. The outward route is rather longer than the return.*

### Parking

OS Map 194 Ref ST7000. Parking area in Church Lane beside the River Piddle.

### Further exploration

Piddletrenthide Church

A small notice in the churchyard points out two early 17th-century headstones to William and Thomas Dumberfield, a family immortalised in Thomas Hardy's novel 'Tess of the D'Urbervilles'.

Follow Church Lane past the church round to a white cottage on the left. Turn left to follow a waymarked route (blue arrow) down a road which soon becomes a grassy track running parallel to the river. Turn left on joining a country lane and then right (waymarked) towards Trent House. On reaching the barns, bear left and shortly cross the river onto a concrete path beside the Piddle Inn. At the main road turn right, soon crossing to go up Tullons Lane (blue arrow). Remain on this lane, which soon becomes a wide grassy bridleway, passing a large barn, until the main bridleway bears right. Here, take the narrow path straight ahead and, at a T-junction of paths, turn left to follow an established bridleway, with Dole's Ash Farm on the right. Cross a narrow lane onto a wide bridleway (waymarked) until you reach the top of the hill, where there is a large barn in a copse and, at the fence, bear left up beside the copse. On the corner, bear slightly left across the field towards a metal gate and follow marker arrows across a field downhill over stiles, eventually following a wide bridleway down into the Plush valley. When you reach the lane, bear left to the village of Plush and the pub.

# Brace of Pheasants (Free House)

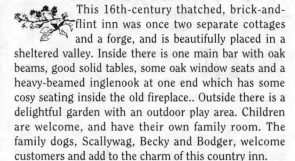 This 16th-century thatched, brick-and-flint inn was once two separate cottages and a forge, and is beautifully placed in a sheltered valley. Inside there is one main bar with oak beams, good solid tables, some oak window seats and a heavy-beamed inglenook at one end which has some cosy seating inside the old fireplace.. Outside there is a delightful garden with an outdoor play area. Children are welcome, and have their own family room. The family dogs, Scallywag, Becky and Bodger, welcome customers and add to the charm of this country inn.

On draught: beers change regularly and may include Wadworth 6X and IPA, Bass, Burton Ale, Guinness, Fosters, Kronenbourg 1664, Addlestone cider. Food: The large selection of dishes includes mushroom and stilton soup (£1.75), ploughman's (from £3.35), steak and kidney pie (£5.85), grilled salmon with lime and ginger butter (£9.25) and wild duck breasts with black cherry sauce (£9.25); times are 12-2pm and 7-10pm.

Telephone: 03004 357 (348357 from July 1993).

From the pub, bear right along the lane, soon to take the waymarked track (Alton Pancras) on the right. As this track bears right to go uphill, take the track off to the left which gradually follows the terracing uphill towards a gate. Go across a field, keeping to the left-hand side, then turn right at the corner to follow the hedge uphill for about 200 yards before crossing a stile (horse-jump) into a huge field. Bear diagonally left across this vast field, heading towards the lower corner, and Piddletrenthide church which will eventually come into view as you progress down into the valley. Cross a wooden gate in the hedge near a small copse and continue downhill on an established track. At the road, turn left and then cross over into Church Lane for the return to your car.

# Bolderwood to Emery Down

~ Approximately 5½ miles ~

*A quiet walk through uncultivated woods and heaths in the New Forest, with two shallow streams to cross. Look out for wild ponies (you can hardly miss them) and snakes.*

**Parking**

OS Map 195 SU2607. Forestry Commission parking area at Millyford Bridge, 11/2 miles west of the A35.

**Further Exploration**

Holiday Hills Reptiliary

Seven open-air enclosures hold native reptiles and amphibians found in the New Forest. Admission free. Leaflet available. Open 8am–8pm daily but closed Oct–Mar during winter hibernation.

From the parking area pass through the wooden barrier to follow the gravel forest track parallel to the stream. Cross the stream and shortly pass through double wooden gates into Holmhill Inclosure, a coniferous plantation. Remain on this track over a small wooden bridge and shortly turn right at a crossways of tracks onto a track that can be muddy. Beyond a small wooden gate, keep ahead on an established narrow path through oak and beech wood, cross a small bridge over a stream and join a track through a clearing. On reaching a wide gravel track turn right and follow it uphill, passing Acres Down car park. Pass Acres Down House, then at a junction of tracks and a house, turn right to follow a sunken track uphill through holly trees. At the top, where it bears left, veer right towards a wooden barrier and follow the track (sometimes muddy) ahead. Shortly, bear off left onto a grassy path downhill then keep left across open heathland. Past a pond to the left the path soon merges with a gravel track. Bear right, pass Crownwood House and eventually reach a lane. Turn right for Emery Down and the pub.

# New Forest Inn (Whitbread)

 This large country inn nestles snugly amid the trees, its yellow-painted exterior a cheerful sight for weary walkers. Inside, the inn is panelled, beamed, and decorated with an assortment of brasses, hunting pictures, guns, lamps and deer antlers. You might want to sit in one of the sections of the garden, or alternatively at one of the tables on the covered patio, under the hanging geraniums. Children and dogs arewelcome, and there are 4 guest bedrooms.

On draught: Whitbread, Strong Country, Flowers, Wadworth 6X, and guest beers, as well as, Guinness, and Murphy's. Food: choice is either from the basic menu or from the daily specials and dishes range from soup (£2.50) and ploughman's (£3.50), to hot dishes with vegetables, perhaps nut roast (£5.75), sauté of veal with paprika (£6.75),or breast of chicken in stilton sauce (£7.50); times are 11–2pm and 6–9.30pm, Sun 12–2pm and 7–9pm.

Telephone: 0703 282329.

 From the inn turn right and follow the gravel track uphill beside the pub to a wooden barrier to join an established track. Head uphill through woodland, pass to the right of Emery Down Reservoir tank and drop down onto another track. Turn right, remaining on the track as it bears left towards the main road. At a crossways of routes turn right uphill, go over the crest and proceed downhill on what can become a very wet and muddy thoroughfare through the wood. Maintain your course on the wide path across intersecting paths and soon reach the perimeter fence to the grounds of Allum Green. Briefly skirt a brick wall, then keep right on the wide path away from the wall and head uphill through bracken, holly, and birch woodland. Gently descend and soon cross over a stream to a wooden barrier and gravel drive. Turn right, then pass between a car park and the Holiday Hills Reptiliary, bearing off left before the main gate onto a grassy track. Follow the perimeter fence to a gate and go up an avenue of trees to a stony track. Turn right and follow the forest track keeping left past a pond to a gate and a lane, Turn right back to the car park.

**New Forest Museum and Visitor Centre, Lyndhurst**
The story of the New Forest, including its history, traditions, character and wildlife, told through an audio-visual show and exhibition displays. Admission charged. Telephone: 0703 283914.

# Froxfield to Steep

≈ Approximately 5 miles ≈

*This undulating walk through beech hangers, across farmland is especially beautiful in spring.*

**Parking**

OS Map 197 Ref SU7327. Near Hangers Way along Cockshott Lane

**Further Exploration**

Steep

The village was the home of the First World War poet Edward Thomas, from 1906-1916. One of his three homes in the village is Berryfield Cottage, next to Ashford Chace. He was killed at the Battle of Arras in 1917

From the car, remain on the track (which can be muddy), ignoring both the Hangers Way route and the path on your left, and head downhill to take the second path on your right through a gate downhill to a lane. Turn left to another lane, and keep left before taking the waymarked path on your right next to a driveway. Cross a stile, and bear right across a field between two telegraph poles marked with yellow arrows. Turn left over a stile, soon to cross another stile, and follow the left-hand edge of the field to a stile. Cross and follow the waymarked path to the right of some old farm buildings, into woodland. Cross the driveway of a house, go back into the wood, and before you meet a track, turn left across a stile, go uphill over the next stile and head across the field towards a stile in the fence on the left. Cross, and when you reach a narrow lane, turn right. At a sharp left-hand bend, take the path on the right, cross a stream by a timbered house and continue up to the pub which is on the right.

# Harrow (Free House)

This is a very pretty two-storey, brick and tiled inn whose two separate bars are simply furnished with wooden tables and benches, tiled floors, huge log fires and stripped pine wall boards. The walls are adorned with old prints of local characters and the cricket team, and there are also a few bookshelves crammed with reading material. Both bars are served from small hatches, with beer dispensed straight from the cask. Children are not allowed inside. Outside, sturdy tables and benches crowd the area in front of the pub, and there is a colourful garden at the back.

On draught: Flowers Original, Strong Country, Boddingtons Best and Bulmer's Original cider. Food: superb, home-cooked meals are served in very generous portions, andthe menu may include soup (£2.10), ploughmans (£3.20), sandwiches (from £1.50), lasagne (£4.75), scotch eggs (£1.20) and huge salads (£6-£7); times are 12-1.45pm and 6.30-9.30pm.

Telephone: (0730) 262685.

**Ashford Chace**
The gardens of this large house are open to the public under the National Gardens Scheme on some Sundays in summer.

Turn right out of the pub, then right again at a road. Follow this uphill to Steep church, and turning right, cross a small playing field into woodland. Emerging from this, cross a stile and keep to the left-hand edge of the field to a road. Bear right and, at a corner near a mill house, take the path on the left, which soon joins another path. Keep left to join another track, and bear right, following this up to a gateway and a lane, with Ashford Chace to the left. Turn left into the lane, then turn right when you reach an established track. Where this bears steeply round to the right, carry on straight ahead following a path uphill through woodland. You will eventually join Cockshott Lane, where you turn right to return to your car.

# Goodworth Clatford to Testcombe

∽ Approximately 6 miles ∽

*A riverside walk along the Anton and Test valleys through gently undulating farmland.*

**Parking**

OS Map 185 Ref SU3642. By the church

**Further Exploration**

The Test Valley abounds in picturesque villages, of which Stockbridge, Wherwell and Longparish are good examples. Winchester, with its great cathedral is a delightful old city and to the west of Andover is the Hawk Conservancy at Weyhill, devoted to birds of prey. Telephone 0264 772252

Walk through the village to a footpath on your left, by Anton Cottage. Follow the right-hand footpath uphill to emerge into a field, with the River Anton on your right. Follow the river bank, pass the sewage works and, just before you reach a gate, turn right to cross a wooden footbridge into a watermeadow, turning right to retrace your steps along the opposite bank, but soon turning left to cross the field, following the line of the fence. Through a gate, turn left onto a bridleway to a belt of trees which marks the start of an abandoned railway cutting. At the gate on your left, turn right across the field to a copse. At a footpath sign, keep straight on up, then turn left to walk along the ridge of the field to emerge into a steep, narrow lane opposite Fullerton Manor. Turn left downhill to the A3057. Alternatively, you can continue on the bridlepath - although it is not a public right of way, and is often used by shooting parties. This path leads round to the right in front of an old bridge to join the lane, where you turn left to reach the A3057. Turn right on to the main road and continue for quarter of a mile to the pub.

# Mayfly (Whitbread)

This pub has an idyllic location, right on the bank of the River Test - Hampshire's most famous trout fishing river - below an old arched bridge. Chairs and tables line its waterfront terrace and inside are spacious bar areas and a conservatory overlooking the river. Its location and excellent buffet bar make this pub very popular , especially in the summer. Children welcome away from the bar.

On draught: Whitbread Best, Strong Country, Flowers Original, Stella Artois and Heineken. Food: very good cold meats and cheeses with a wide choice of salads are what this pub is famous for. There is usually also a hot dish of the day. Prices range from around £2.50 to £4.20; food is available all day to 9pm.

Telephone: 0264 860283.

On leaving the pub, cross the bridge, then turn left towards Chilbolton. Walk along this pretty, wooded lane for about half a mile until you see on your left a little fenced square of grass with a garden seat overlooking the River Test. A waymarked footpath (green arrow on white background) leads between high fences to a playing field. Cross by the sports hut to a track leading to your left and pass an old thatched cottage onto common land. Keep right around the common, following the green arrows, across a bridge and straight on across the common to two more footbridges which bring you out on to a country lane. Turn left and very soon, take the footpath on your right leading up a steep bank to two stiles. Take the left-hand stile and, keeping the hedge on your left, walk round the edge of the field until you reach the very top. Here, take the path on your right leading between tall hedges, and follow it along until it bends left downhill through some bushes and across a neck of the field below to a gate on to the main road. Cross over to the field path opposite and walk along the edge of the field to a gate which leads you back on to the path by the River Anton. Retrace your steps to Goodworth Clatford.

# Tichborne to Cheriton

~ Approximately 5 miles ~

*A peaceful walk through undulating farmland and pasture along the tranquil Itchen valley.*

**Parking**

OS Map 185 Ref SU 569302
Tichborne church

**Further Exploration**

Tichborne

The Tichborne Dole, an old tradition originated during the reign of Henry I involves local residents receiving a bag of flour from the owners of Tichborne Park. A callous promise from Sir Roger Tichborne to his bedridden wife that she should provide funds for the needy, as much land as she could crawl round: the 20 acres she managed to encompass is known as the Crawls.

From the church parking area walk down the lane past the Old School House and take the trackway off to the right. When this merges into a field, keep left parallel to the hedge to reach a stile, then carry straight on at first break in the hedgerow onto a narrow path at the field's edge. Cross the stile in the hedgerow to the left and head diagonally right across a large field towards a barn. Cross another stile, bear right and follow an established trackway (can be muddy) up the valley passing three barns before reaching a metal gate beside the track. Enter the field and keep left following the fence downhill with good views back down the valley towards the Itchen valley. Go uphill and enter a woodland via a small wooden gate and remain on the often muddy twisting path through the wood. On leaving the wood bear left to follow a farm road and trackway soon to pass through 'Hill Houses', a tiny hamlet of thatched cottages. Go downhill following the road towards Cheriton and on nearing the first house at the base of the hill cross the stile on the right and head across the playing field and children's play area. After a further stile keep to the left-hand side of the field to join a concrete path leading into a small cul-de-sac. Bear right and you will soon have the welcome sight of the pub.

# The Flower Pots (Free House)

Originally built as a farmhouse in 1840, the Flower Pots epitomises how a homely village inn should be. The plain brick exterior hides a very friendly welcome within its two simple bars. The cosy saloon bar has a sofa, among other chairs, in which to relax and a small log fire; the spotlessly clean public bar being furnished with various wooden settles and chairs around pine tables, all laid out in front of a warm open fire. An unusual feature here is the glass-topped 27-foot-deep well. There is a children's room and a garden.

On draught: Archers Village Bitter, Ballards Best, Hop Back Summer Lightning, guest beer, Fosters, Guinness, Bulmers Original cider. Food: hearty, value-for-money bar snacks include chilli (£2.65), with garlic bread (£2.95), beef stew (£3.30), sweet and sour chicken (£3.30), jacket potatoes with various fillings (from £1.60), ham sandwich (£1.40), toasted sandwiches (from £1.30); times are 12-2pm and 7-9.30pm (Sun12-2.30pm, 7-9pm). Telephone 0962 771318.

**St Andrews Church**
The Tichborne family were Catholic so the parish church retains a Catholic side chapel with memorials to various members. The church is nearly 900 years old and contains some fine box pews.

**Cheriton**
The River Itchen flows through this tranquil village with a green and some fine thatched cottages which is often voted Hampshire's Best Kept Village. Near the village is Hinton Ampner, off the A272, a house with a lovely garden, now belonging to the National Trust. Telephone 0962 771305

On leaving the pub retrace your steps across the playing field back to the lane and cross over to follow the waymarked 'Itchen Way'. The path tracks the bank of the River Itchen crossing five stiles before passing in front of Cheriton Mill. On joining a quiet lane turn left and follow this to Sevington Farm, then take the trackway off to the right opposite the farm entrance. Cross over the River Itchen and climb a stile into a large field. Follow the path diagonally left towards a gateway into woodland, eventually passing through this narrow woodland via two stiles. Keep to the left-hand side of the next field and soon join the driveway to Tichborne House. Cross this to join a road which bears left, passing Tichborne Pottery and crossing the river again, before joining a lane. Turn left opposite Park Cottage and follow the lane up through the thatched village of Tichborne. On reaching the sharp left-hand bend, bear right to join a narrow path uphill which takes you back to the church parking area.

# Swallowcliffe Down to Ebbesbourne Wake

~ Approximately 6 miles ~

*A chalk downland and valley walk, through open meadows and along ancient an ancient ox-droving route, with an abundance of wild flowers and wildlife such as hares, skylarks, red-legged partridges and pheasants.*

**Parking**

OS Map 184 Ref ST9625. Top of Swallowcliffe/Middle Downs - an old ox drove off a country lane.

Walk westwards along the ox drove towards White Sheet Hill. Shortly after you emerge from the trees, follow a path to your left, waymarked with a blue arrow. With a track merging from the right, follow the footpath downhill. The path keeps to the edge of the wood, through a gate and on to a track, down to Norington, a large medieval-looking manor house. Cross the concrete drive and pass between the farm outbuildings, bearing right at a fence, towards the front of the house. Cross the stile next to the fuel pump and continue across the grazing land towards some houses. After the next stile, cross the drive and follow the footpath to the left of a stream, towards Alvediston church. At the stile, cross the lane where there is a signpost to Ebbesbourne. Walk up the drive towards the church and, after about 100 yards, go through the waymarked gate into a field. Cross the field and pass through another gate on to a track and continue past the cottages at West End. On reaching a lane, cross the bridge and follow the lane signposted to Ebbesbourne Wake. At a fork, bear left, then at a path by some white railings, head off to the right, up to the church and down into the main village street, bearing right.

THE HORSESHOE

# The Horseshoe (Free House)

This attractive country pub has a pleasant, well-kept garden with numerous picnic benches overlooking the quiet, steep-sided Ebble valley. Inside, a central bar serves two rooms; the snug, a tiny room decorated with prints and curiosities on the walls; and the public bar with beams, lanterns, a vast collection of farm tools and a large open fire. A third room, with a wood-burning stove, houses the small, neat restaurant. Children are welcome in the eating areas, and the garden is very safe for youngsters.

On draught: Wadworth 6X, Ringwood Best and Old Thumper, Adnams Broadside, Beamish, Carlsberg. Food: home-made soup (£1.95), ploughman's (from £3.50), and sandwiches (from £2.25)are the staple fare, and there is also a hot dish or so of the day - for example - steak and kidney pie (£5.25). Puddings are home-made and include fruit pies and crumbles (£2.25). Traditional Sunday lunch at three courses for £7.95 is good value; times are 12-2pm, restaurant 7-9.30pm (except Mon) and for Sun lunch (booking essential).

Telephone: 0722 780474.

### Further Exploration

Ebbesbourne Wake is a quaint village, very quiet and apparently free from the rigours of modern-day pressures - no main road, little if any modern building, no sign of new construction. The village consists mainly of thatched cottages backing on quiet lanes and nestling around the church and the pub.

Turn right out of the pub, then turn left downhill past some thatched cottages. At a left-hand bend, take the path to your right, crossing a small footbridge. Cross a stile on your left and keep left, crossing the field diagonally up to a stile in the hedge (not immediately visible). Cross the lane and the stile opposite and walk up the field. At the first gate on your left, turn right on the bridleway across the field. At the other side, go through the gap in the fence towards the next gate. Through this, follow the track in the grass down a steep bank to where it joins an established track. Follow this track up through the centre of the valley, then bear right through the thicket up to the valley head. Emerging from the thicket, bear left through gate on to an established track. Turn left again and follow this track along the edge of two fields before crossing a stile to join the old ox drove. Keep left and follow the path back to the car.

# King Alfred's Tower to Stourton

~ Approximately 5½ miles ~

*An enjoyable ramble
through the Stourhead
Estate, through the
varied scenery of park,
farm, and woodland.*

**Parking:**
O. S. Map 183 Ref ST 7435
National Trust car park at King
Alfred's Tower.

**Further Exploration**
Stourhead House and
Gardens
Henry Hoare I, banker son of a
Lord Mayor of London, built
Stourhead in the 1720s. It
contains fine furniture and
paintings and carved woodwork
by Grinling Gibbons. The superb
landscaped gardens were laid
out between 1741 and 1780 and
include lakes, temples and rare
trees and plants. They are
especially attractive in early
spring when the daffodils are in
bloom. The lake is edged with
magnificient rhododendrons,
beeches and tulip trees.
Telephone (0747) 840348.

King Alfred's Tower
This red-brick folly was built in
1772 by Flitcroft at the edge of
the estate and stands 160ft high.
There are fine views over the
neighbouring counties of
Somerset and Dorset.

From the car park head away from King Alfred's Tower along a clear track, parallel to the lane. Ignore the first woodland track right, taking the second beside the 'Tower' fingerpost. Join a wide track and head downhill through woodland. Keep to the defined track, which eventually levels out to a gate and open country. Bear left with the track around the base of woodland to another gate; the site of Tucking Mill and its lake lie along the track to the right. Pass through the small wooden gate, continue over the rise and shortly join a gravel track leading to a house on your left. Keep ahead following this downhill, bear left through a gate and pass below the dam of the main lake in Stourhead Gardens. With Turner's Paddock Lake on your right, follow the track round to a lane. Turn left, pass under a rocky arched bridge and below the Temple of Apollo into Stourton village. The entrance to the gardens is on the left by the cross and green, the pub a little further along the lane on the right.

From the pub walk through the courtyard and car park towards Stourhead House. Cross the lane, enter the old turnstile beside the main gate and follow the path past old Spanish chestnut trees to a kissing gate. Remain on the path with Stourhead House to the left, then bear left through parkland to a small gate and lane. Climb the stile across the lane and head slightly left (north) over arable land to a stile in a wire fence beyond the rise. Cross the stile and keep ahead along the fence, over a double stile and field to another stile, then drop down onto a sunken green lane. Turn left along this old coach road to a metalled lane and junction. Cross, following the lane towards King Alfred's Tower. On reaching some beech trees, you can take a path through the trees, parallel to the lane. To your left, Six Wells Bottom comes into view and the obelisk (St Peter's Pump) marking the site of the original springs of the River Stour. Remain on the path back to the car park.

# Spread Eagle Inn (Free House)

This delightful 18th-century inn is owned by the National Trust, whose shop and tearooms occupy part of the same courtyard. Popular with visitors to Stourhead, it is simply yet tastefully furnished with a collection of captain's chairs, oak benches, attractive fabrics and interesting prints on the walls. There is a huge inglenook fireplace in the main bar and a woodburner warms the pleasant lounge. Children are welcome.

On draught: Ashvine Bitter, Bass, a guest ale, Tennants Pilsner and, Lowenbrau, . Food: good-value bar food ranges from home-made soup (£1.90) and ploughman's (from £3), to daily specials such as Huntingdon pie (£4.75) and fisherman's pie (£4.75). Tempting puddings may include treacle pudding and custard (£2.85) or trifle (£1.95). Morning coffee and afternoon cream teas are available; otherwise times are 11.45am-2pm and 6-9pm, Sun 12-2pm and 7-9.30pm.

Telephone: 0747 840587.

# Derry Hill to Lacock

### ~ Approximately 6½ miles ~

*A pleasant ramble
across farmland
through the Avon
valley, taking in a
National Trust village
and panoramic views.*

**Parking**

OS Map 173 Ref ST9571.
Side road off junction of A342
and A4, half a mile from Derry
Hill

Take the road marked `Naishes Hill '
uphill to a stone house beyond a
cattle grid. Turn right in front of the
house onto a track and pass through three metal gates
before reaching a concrete path. Go straight across it
and follow the track through a gate and across a field to
another gate. Follow the right-hand edge of the field,
and once across the field, soon drop down through a
small thicket to a wooden stile. Follow yellow arrows
around the base of the hill and go through a small gate
on the right. Pass through another gate and follow the
path along the raised bank of a disused canal, with the
River Avon to the right. Cross a stile into a wooded area
(path can be muddy) then, emerging into a field, bear
right and follow the hedge down towards some
buildings. Go through the gap in the corner and cross a
field to two green metal stiles in the hedge, then follow
the established path down to a lane. Go over a stile
ahead and bear left toward another one near the river
bridge. Cross the bridge, turn left, then follow the
metalled path between houses and across a field to a
swing gate. Turn left and cross a stream into Lacock.
Turn right at the church, then left past the Carpenters
Arms to the Red Lion at the end of the street.

# Red Lion (Wadworth)

The austere Georgian façade hides a rambling bar, furnished in traditional country style and warmed by open log fires. Prints, old plates, agricultural implements and a fine collection of stuffed birds decorate the interior. Children are very welcome.

On draught: Wadworth 6X, IPA and Old Timer. Food: the menu includes good soups, pies, casseroles and delicious puddings at prices ranging from £2.05 to £6.

Telephone: 024973 363.

Turn right from the pub and walk uphill to the church, taking the driveway opposite it towards a gatehouse. Bear right in front of the gatehouse, cross two stiles and turn right to follow the edge of the field, with Bowden House and gardens to the left. Cross a stile and a small gravel car park and head across the parkland towards the black barn ahead. Cross the stile beside a cattle grid and follow the road past a farm. At a T-junction, turn left onto a quiet lane past a stone barn, and turn right along Ash Hill farm driveway, soon to follow the waymarked route ('Pewsham') downhill on a private road. Cross a cattle grid, pass through a copse, and cross two more grids before, at the base of the hill, turning right onto your outward route and following this back to the car.

**Further exploration**

Lacock Abbey

Set in the carefully preserved village of 14th-18th-century houses, the Abbey was the venue for a series of innovative photographic experiments by William Fox Talbot which led to the world's first negative to be made in 1835. A museum devoted to him is housed in an old barn. Telephone 024973 227.

# Harting Down to Hooksway

∽ Approximately 6½ miles ∽

*A beautiful walk, offering panoramic views across the Sussex landscape, along the South Downs Way and quiet woodland paths.*

**Parking**
OS Map 197 Ref SU7918 Large car park on top of Harting Down, off B2141

Take the South Downs Way on the right, heading east. Keep to this path to a multi-sign oak post. Climb straight up to the top of Beacon Hill. Carry straight on downhill and through a field, then bear right and follow the South Downs Way. Keep straight on at the next junction and soon the path bends to the left and goes between first a hedge and the woods, and then two fields. On reaching a track, bear left, so on turning right along a broad track with Buriton farm to the right. On joining a second path, take the lower path on the right and then bear right again onto another signposted path. This path keeps straight on to a broad track, which leads you down to Hooksway and the pub.

## Royal Oak (Free House)

Nestling in a hollow, at the end of a lane, this rustic pub is a welcome sight after the breezy walk across the top of the Downs. Inside, there are two open fires and rough flagstones in its two simply furnished bars. Low ceilings with a few beams, and stools around the bar, provide a welcoming atmosphere in which to enjoy a good meal. The garden contains a climbing frame for children, who are also welcome inside.

On draught: Ballard's Best, Gibbs Mew Bishop's Tipple, Gales HSB, Ruddles Best, Ringwood Old Thumper and Guinness. Food: a varied menu includes ploughman's (from £2.80), jacket potatoes (from £2.40), venison pie (£4.25), chilli (£3.85) and tagliatelle (£3.85). Desserts include banoffi pie, cheesecake and gateau (all at £1.80); times are 12-2pm and 7-9.30pm. There is a restaurant which also serves afternoon teas.
Telephone: 024359 257.

Turn right out of the pub and follow the metalled lane uphill. Before reaching the top, bear right onto a broad track and at a T-junction, turn right. Before a bungalow on the left, leave the track, cross a stile on the left and follow the waymarked path across a field by a fence, and then join a metalled track, bearing right. Keep right, with Telegraph House on your left, and once past the large house, take the path on the right up to a gate. Keep to your left along the path for about quarter of a mile and, just before the end of the field on the right, bear left (signposted) downhill into woodland. At the bottom of the hill, go straight on at a junction and head uphill, bearing right at the top. In a short distance, take the path signposted to the right and, at the end of the woods, bear left through a kissing gate onto an arrowed path between woodland and open grassland. Bear left at a junction of paths. With the road in sight, turn right along the track through the woods to the car park.

# Firle Beacon to Alciston

⌘ Approximately 6 miles ⌘

*A downland walk following the South Downs Way with fine views over the Sussex Weald into Kent.*

**Parking**

OS Map 198 Ref TQ4605
Viewpoint near Firle Beacon.

**Further Exploration**

Alciston has been known as the forgotten village since its population fled before the ravages of the Black Death, leaving a 13th-century church and 14th-century Alciston Court. Of particular note is the tithe barn, said to be the longest in the country. On Good Friday, traditional village skipping takes place at the Rose Cottage Inn.

**Charleston Farmhouse**

This former home of Clive and Vanessa Bell was an important artistic focus for the members of the 'Bloomsbury Group'.and visitors included Virginia and Leonard Woolf, Duncan Grant, TS Eliot, EM Forster, Roger Fry and Lytton Strachey. Charleston is a remarkable monument to the creative achievements of Bell, Grant and other artists and the last surviving complete example of their domestic decorative work. Telephone: 032183 265.

Follow the signpost eastwards for the South Downs Way. The wide, grassy downland path leads up to Firle Beacon and past a farm, another car park, and up onto Bostal Hill where various tumuli are visible on the ground. Where the path meets a gate and a track running south (at the end of the fencing, about half a mile from the second car park), bear diagonally left towards the edge of the Downs. Locate a stile, cross it and follow the path off the edge of the Downs, heading towards Alciston. On reaching the metalled road, follow it for quarter of a mile to the pub.

Turn left out of the pub and follow the road until, before reaching the main road, you reach and cross a stile on your left, located at the rear of a small drive. Follow arrows across a small stream to a lane, turn left and then right, and follow the concrete driveway. Continue straight past the cottage through the gates, reaching a driveway and sign for Charleston Farmhouse. Pass in front of the house and remain on marked footpaths and stiles, passing beneath Firle Tower on your right, to join a track beside two cottages. Cross the stile immediately ahead and cross Firle Park, following the arrows. Pass in front of Firle House and through the gate onto a road into Firle village. Bear left at the main lane, past the church, then continue straight on through a farm and follow the footpath up along the edge of Firle Plantation (very steep ascent) to rejoin the South Downs Way a short distance from the car park.

## Rose Cottage (Free House)

Nestling at the base of the South Downs, this well-run little cottage has cosy bars adorned with artefacts such as harnesses, traps, thatcher blades and other ironware. A few stuffed birds, a talking parrot, wheel-backed chairs, church pews with cushions, and open fires, combine to create a relaxed atmosphere. There is also a non-smoking section. Outside, there is a small paddock with chickens and a duckpond, and a covered seating area. Walkers are very welcome and children are allowed in the eating area and restaurant.

On draught: Harveys Best, Young's Bitter. Food: dishes are served in generous helpings: soup (from £1.95), various ploughman's (£3.50), rabbit pie (£4.10), vegetarian nut loaf (£4.95), pancakes (£5.25) and steak (£7.25); times are 12-2pm (Sun1.30pm) and 7-10pm. Telephone: 0323 870377.

### Firle

Once a feudal village, Firle is dominated by Firle Place. Owned by the Gage family since the15th century, it houses a magnificent collection of Sèvres porcelain, fine English and French furniture and galleries containing paintings by Van Dyck, Gainsborough and Reynolds. St Peter's Church dates from 14th century and preserves a Norman door; records of its vicars go as far back as 1197
Telephone: 0273 858335

# Piltdown to Fletching

~ Approximately 4 miles ~

*A gentle ramble across
the farmland of the
Sussex Weald.*

**Parking**

OS Map 198 Ref TQ4422
Parking area beside a small lake,
south of A272 on Piltdown
Common

**Further Exploration**

**Sheffield Park Gardens**
This is beautiful parkland
covering 200 acres, with five
lakes, a superb collection of
trees, landscaped by Capability
Brown in 1775.
Telephone: 0825 790655.

**Bluebell Railway and
Museum**
Located close to Sheffield Park
this five-mile-long revived steam
railway line runs through
woodland. Part of the station is a
museum with a large collection
of locomotives and carriages.
Telephone 082572 3777.

From the parking area turn left, walk along the road beside the golf course and turn left along a track opposite a cottage. Once on the golf course, bear left round the tee area, then head directly across, skirting a green, and soon joining a path bearing left towards a large house called Cogans. Keep to the right of the house through a small copse onto a driveway, bear right and follow it to the main road. Turn right, cross over (with great care) and bear left into the second driveway leading to a business area. Bear right onto scrubland just before the main yard entrance, then join an established path through a bracken-covered common. Turn left onto a driveway, pass in front of Mallingdown Farm and go through two metal gates following a waymarked route (yellow arrows) across fields and stiles. After crossing a footbridge, go straight across a field, cross another stile then, ignoring the stile to the left, cross the metal stile in the left-hand corner of the next field to follow a path to the right of a metal silo into the churchyard. Join the main grassy path past the church into the village, turn right at the road and the pub lies on the left.

Return along the lane, bearing left round the church and past the school. Continue on the road for some distance and climb the stile in the hedge on your right just after Denniker Cottage. Bear downhill, keeping to the right of a clump of trees to a stile, and follow the arrowed route across a soft-fruit-picking area to a gate, then across two fields via stiles to join the main road in Grisling Common. Cross the road, turn left and walk along the pavement, past the pub and post office, then turn right onto the lane back to the lake.

# Griffin Inn (Free House)

 This is a relaxing and very welcoming village local, with a beamed main bar and open fireplace and comfortable seating. In summer, you can eat al fresco in the pleasant garden while enjoying rolling Sussex views. Children are welcome in the family room.

On draught: Harveys Best, Hall and Woodhouse Tanglefoot and Badger Best, King & Barnes, Tennent's Pilsner and Extra, Strongbow cider. Food: daily specials may include spiced parsnip and apple soup (£2.50), fresh salmon fishcakes with dill mayonnaise (£5.50), game pie (£5.50). Puddings (£3.25) include treacle tart, banoffi pie and fresh fruit meringue. There is also a children's menu and a separate restaurant menu; times are 12-2.15pm and 7-9.30pm.

Telephone: 082572 2890.

# Lickfold to Henley
~ Approximately 7 miles ~

*Although some parts of this Sussex walk are steep and for boggy stretches wellingtons or boots are essential, there are rewarding views and very few other walkers about.*

**Parking**

OS Map 197 Ref SU9225. On edge of Lickfold Green near an old red telephone box and a post box in a wall.

At Lickfold Green you will see some farm buildings. Take the footpath signposted north. At two five-barred gates, take the left-hand gate and bear right to follow the sign to the next gate, and to two more gates by a footpath sign. Take the right-hand gate and walk to a stile. Cross and go down into a wood. At a footpath sign, bear left, cross the next stile, and aim for the stile on the left of the field. Here, turn right across a stream, continue to a farm track, turn left, and shortly go through a gate on the right. Follow the edge of the wood round to pass through the gate in the corner of the field. Keep straight to the next two gates and head for the barn at the top of the field. Over a five-barred gate, turn left into a road, and past the farm and a house, go through a five-barred gate into a field, keeping to the left. Follow the signs through the valley to a road, turn right and, once through a pair of gates, ignore the sign pointing through the woods, but continue for a short distance to a sign to the left, next to a field marked 'Private'. Follow this across two stiles and along a grassy path to a small bridge on the right, to go uphill to a track. Here, at the sign, bear right, then turn right at the next waymarked path. Follow this to a T-junction with a wide track, turn right, climb a gate and keep ahead to a road where you turn left for Henley and the pub.

# Duke of Cumberland Arms
# (Free House)

This attractive 15th-century building is set above the road. Inside, the bar, with its low, wood-beamed ceiling and red-tiled floor, is warmed by log fires at either end. comfortably sized wooden tables and benches are surrounded by paintings, photos and some antique clocks and cupboards. There are several tables and benches in the substantial garden, with good views on fine days, and a pond nearby is well stocked with trout that are available on the menu.

On draught: Theakston Old Peculier, King & Barnes Sussex and Festive, Fuller's ESB, Carlsberg, Hacker Pschorr, Farmhouse cider. Food: bar snacks, available lunchtimes and evenings every day, range from soup, sandwiches and ploughman's with either cheese (from £2.80), or Cumberland sausage (from £3.30), to dishes like fresh dressed crab (£4.60) and half-lobster and salad (£8.50). Full lunch and evening menus are also available (booking essential in busy periods) every day except Sun lunch when only bar snacks are served.

Telephone: 0428 652280.

Return to the footpath by the phone box opposite the pub car park. Follow this for a short distance, turning left at a footpath sign. Keep on this path as it winds round and goes uphill again, eventually going into a wood. Then take the path up a steep hill, and at the next track crossing, bear left. Here the track runs steeply downhill to a better defined track where you bear right. At a lane, turn left and continue past a few houses, down the hill for about 1/4 mile until, shortly after the road bends to the left, you take the footpath signed right, by the fir copse. At the next signpost, keep straight on, to come to another sign where you turn left and, on reaching the woods, take the path signed to the right. At a house on the right, take the path to its left leading to a road where you turn right for Lickfold Green to return to your car.

# Penshurst to Chiddingstone

~ Approximately 6 miles ~

*A beautiful Wealden Walk through peaceful meadows, woodland and parkland.*

**Parking**

OS Map 188 Ref TQ5243. Penshurst village

**Further Exploration**

**Penshurst Place**

Originally a medieval manor house, Penshurst was converted into a grand estate by the Sidney family in the 16th century and has connections with the dramatist Ben Jonson and Lady Pembroke, sister of the famous poet and soldier Sir Phillip Sidney who was born here in 1554. The chestnut beamed great hall is the oldest and finest such structure in the country, and the state rooms are lavishly furnished. Among the other attractions are a toy museum, Tudor-style gardens and a nature trail. Telephone 0892 870307.

**Chiddingstone Castle**

This 17th-century castle contains Stewart and Jacobite paintings, Egyptian and Oriental antiquities, and a collection of Japanese lacquer and swords. Telephone 0892 870347

From the village centre, follow the B2176 north past Fir Tree Tea Rooms on the left and Penshurst Place on the right. In a short distance, take the lane on the left leading to Salmans Farm. Cross the River Eden and bear right onto a bridleway. Through a farmyard, turn right onto the lane, soon to follow a waymarked footpath on the left into mixed woodland. Ignore the track that turns sharp left to a farm gate, instead turn right by a waymarked stile and walk along the edge of a field to a stile in the left-hand corner, then diagonally left across the field to yet another stile. Follow the path down to a quiet lane and then bear left into Chiddingstone and the pub.

Return along the lane, bearing left, pass the oast house and Larkins Brewery, and follow the lane down to the bridge over the river. Cross, then climb a stile on the right and bear right across a field to cross a small wooden footbridge. Bear right to cross a metal bridge over a stream and follow the yellow markers over stiles and fields to a road. Bear right for a short distance, then take the waymarked path through a farm, keeping the farmhouse to the left. Cross a hop field and a meadow to a gate, and join a quiet lane beside a railway bridge. Bear right and follow the lane to a road junction. Turn left and almost immediately right, onto an arrowed footpath into woodland. Take the path to the right, and keep right at the next fork. Remain on this path to a stile, cross it, bear right, then left down to another stile and enter the beautiful parkland of Penshurst Place, heading downhill through an avenue of oak trees. Two-thirds of the way down, bear right and head towards a stile, then with the lake on the left, head towards another stile and sign ahead, then straight towards a large house. Cross the drive and leave the park at the church. Through the churchyard, turn right on the road back to the village.

# Castle Inn (Free House)

Owned by the National Trust, the building dates from 1420, but became an inn in 1752. It is tile hung from roof to ground, with latticed windows overlooking the peaceful churchyard. Inside, the main bar has been modernised well, with settles around tables, sturdy cushioned wall-settles, oak beams and floor, and a fine open stone fireplace. The public bar is simpler, with wall-settles and a few chairs, and has a darts board, shove-ha'penny and dominoes. There is a separate restaurant and an enclosed garden with a small bridge across a pool and rockery to a lawn with sturdy picnic benches. Children are welcome in the eating area of the bar.

On draught: Larkins, Harveys Sussex, Shepherd Neame Master Brew, guest ales, Beamish, Carlsberg and Hurliman. Food: good, appetising bar food includes open sandwiches (from £3.25), ploughman's (from £4.50), filled jacket potatoes (from £3.75),and main courses like beef and vegetable curry (£4.75), and salads (£6.55). Desserts may include Dutch apple slice and cream (£2.35) and Amourette Cointreau ice-cream (£2.35); times are 11-2.30pm and 6-10.30pm.

Telephone: 0892 870247.

# Egerton to Pluckley

~ Approximately 4½ miles ~

*A pleasant and easy walk taking in a mixture of open farmland and pasture with fine views of the North Downs and across the Weald of Kent.*

**Parking**

OS Mapm 189 Ref TQ 9047
Egerton Church or village hall

Turn left from the church and follow the road towards Stonebridge Green, then turn right through a gate, opposite Court Lodge Farm, onto a track. At the end of the track keep on ahead between two fields to a hedge. Keep the hedge on your right as far as the bottom right-hand corner of the field and pass through it, turning left and shortly entering an orchard.Follow its edge left-handed to the bottom corner, then pass through a gap in the hedge onto a bridlepath. Turn right and follow this path to a narrow lane. Turn right, then left onto another track and follow it to the B2077. The remains of St Mary's Church nestling in among the farm buildings of Chart Court lie to the left. Turn right here along the road into Pluckley and turn left, signed Bethersden, to find the pub on the left, next to the church.

# Black Horse (Whitbread)

In winter open log fires welcome customers into this old inn, reputed to date from 1470. The low-ceilinged bar has comfortable cushioned wall settles and stools and interesting tapestries decorate the walls. Children are welcome in the restaurant area. A large attractive garden has sturdy picnic tables.

On draught: Fuller's London Pride, Marston's Pedigree, Fremlins Bitter, Harveys Sussex Bitter, Brakspear Bitter, Murphy's, Guinness, Stella Artois and Heineken. Food: the menu ranges from soup (£1.65) and salads (from £4.35), to mixed grill (£7.50), and roast duck in orange sauce (£9.50) and there are daily specials for around £4-£5 as well. Puddings may include sherry trifle and apple and blackberry pie (both £1.85); times are 12-2pm and 7-9.30pm.

Telephone 0233 840256.

Retrace your steps to the B-road, turn left and head downhill a little way before turning right along a track between two houses, waymarked 'Greensand Way'. Beyond a gate, turn left through another gate and cross a field diagonally right to a gate and descend to Elvey Farm (yellow markers). Pass through two more gates into the farmyard, keeping the farmhouse and oast houses to your right. Cross the farm road, pass through a double iron gate, then cross the stile ahead and bear diagonally left to climb another stile at the lower end of the field. Once over the stream turn right along the edge of the field and follow the Greensand Way markers over several stiles to Greenhill Farm. Go through the iron gate and turn left along the farm track to a road. Turn right uphill, shortly to take a signed footpath on the left, then descend some steps into a field and follow its right-hand edge to a stile in the corner. Beyond a further stile the path leads you to Stone Hill Farm, where, on reaching the road, turn right uphill, shortly to take a footpath on the left, opposite a new bungalow, through a small estate back to the village centre.

## Further Exploration

### Pluckley

The village is renowned as the most haunted village in Kent and the Black Horse itself is said to have two ghosts. The buildings in the village have unusual-shaped windows of an unusual shape, known locally as Dering windows, after an incident in the Civil War when a member of the Dering family used such a window to escape from the Roundheads. The author H.E. Bates lived in the area and based his book the 'Darling Buds of May' around the village, where the popular television series was also filmed.

### Leeds Castle

Described as 'the loveliest castle in the world' it is built on two islands in the middle of a lake and set in 500 acres of landscaped parkland. It was once a royal palace for Henry VIII and subsequent royals for over three centuries. Now open to the public, it has beautiful pictures and other treasures.
Telephone: 0622 765400.

# Hollingbourne to Ringlestone

~ Approximately 5½ miles ~

*A rural walk across farmland affording super views from the North Downs.*

**Parking**

OS Map 178, 188 and 189 Ref TQ8455

Outside Hollingbourne Church.

From the church walk up the road, turning right by the Dirty Habit pub onto a metalled lane. Where the lane gives way to a bridleway, bear left gradually uphill along a gravel track. Follow the path on the right (yellow markers) uphill through a small copse and along the edge of a field to a stile. Keep to the left-hand path through the edge of a beech wood uphill to a stile, and cross a large field heading between a cottage and a concrete water reservoir to a lane. Cross the lane into a field and head diagonally right on a path (not waymarked) passing down the left-hand side of a copse to two stiles and bear half-right across another field to join a lane near a house. Turn left and shortly turn right along a lane signposted 'Camping - tents only', past the entrance to a house on the right, uphill and over the stile on the right, following the route across a field to another stile. Bear diagonally left across the next field to a stile in the corner next to a wood, then follow the path through a wooden gate onto a track down to a lane and the pub.

# Ringlestone Inn (Free House)

Built in 1533, this was originally a hospice for the monks travelling along the Pilgrim's Way. The original brickwork and beams are complemented by antique furniture, flagstone floors and some unusual additions, such as the small bread oven tucked away in the main room, and the 17th-century sideboard behind the bar. Outside, there are picnic tables. Children are welcome.

On draught: there is not space enough here to list all of the beers offered, but they include Felinfoel Double Dragon, Archers Headbanger, Goacher's Maidstone Ale and 1066, Mitchell's, Shepherd Neame Bishop's Finger and Spitfire, two stouts, six lagers, two ciders and 24 English fruit country wines. Food: prices range from abut 95p for a jacket potato to £4.25 for a hot dish, but the big attraction is the hot and cold lunch buffet that often includes a range of salads, savoury fish bake, lasagne, spiced chicken casserole, and lamb and Stilton pies (from around £3); times are 12-2pm and 7-9.30pm.

Telephone: 0622 859900.

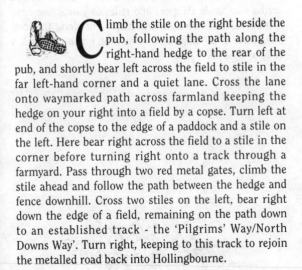

Climb the stile on the right beside the pub, following the path along the right-hand hedge to the rear of the pub, and shortly bear left across the field to stile in the far left-hand corner and a quiet lane. Cross the lane onto waymarked path across farmland keeping the hedge on your right into a field by a copse. Turn left at end of the copse to the edge of a paddock and a stile on the left. Here bear right across the field to a stile in the corner before turning right onto a track through a farmyard. Pass through two red metal gates, climb the stile ahead and follow the path between the hedge and fence downhill. Cross two stiles on the left, bear right down the edge of a field, remaining on the path down to an established track - the 'Pilgrims' Way/North Downs Way'. Turn right, keeping to this track to rejoin the metalled road back into Hollingbourne.

# Frittenden to Three Chimneys

~ Approximately 4 miles ~

*A peaceful level walk across the pastureland of the Kentish Weald*

**Parking**
OS Map 188 Ref TQ8140
Frittenden church (along the roadside)

**Further Exploration**
Sissinghurst Castle Garden (National Trust)
The gardens surrounding the remains of this tudor mansion are among the most attractive and popular in England. Different areas of Vita Sackville West's famous garden are planted according to a theme or season - for example the White Garden and the Cottage Garden - and there is also an old-fashioned rose garden.
Telephone 0580 712850.

From the church, head towards the village centre, turning right opposite the village school onto a metalled path beside the driveway to Hill Farm. In a short distance, before some houses on the right follow the waymarked route across two stiles and a driveway, and follow yellow arrows over many stiles, across pastureland and through an orchard to a narrow lane. Turn left, shortly turning right beside Chanceford Farm and across a driveway, to a stile. Climb this and the stile ahead, then follow the left-hand edge of a large field, passing a small lake on the left. Cross two more stiles and follow the markers towards the farm ahead. Disregard the small iron gate ahead and pass through the five-bar iron gate to the left (waymarked), then turn right into another field and follow the fence to another gate on the right leading to the farm. Cross the grass between the pond and the house, towards a farm building and join a concrete drive, then a track and descend down through a gate to a bridge across a brook. Follow yellow arrows across four fields via gates and stiles to join a lane near some houses. Go straight and turn right along the road signposted to Sissinghurst, remaining on this for half a mile to the pub.

# Three Chimneys (Free house)

This is a classic country pub with its original small-roomed layout and old-fashioned furnishings still intact. Low beams, open fires and a mix of country chairs provide a warm atmosphere in which to enjoy a relaxed drink or meal. There is a simple public bar, a cosy and intimate main bar, and a garden room which is popular with families. There is also a good sheltered garden.

On draught: Wadworth 6X, Goacher's, Fremlins, Adnams, Marston's Pedigree, Harveys Best (and Old Ale in winter), Stella Artois, Biddenden cider. Food: a menu is chalked up daily and consists of tasty and interesting dishes, including home-made soup (£2.15), hearty snacks of bread, cheese and home-made chutney (£3), spinach and ham mousse (£2.80), scallop and mushroom pie (£5.50) and cold honey-roast chicken (£6.25) There is also a good choice of vegetarian dishes. Puddings range from buttered brazil cheesecake to grape and banana pavlova (both £2.75); times are 12-2pm and 7-10pm.

Telephone: 0580 291472.

From the pub, bear right down a quiet lane and climb the stile on the right after passing the drive-way to Bettenham Barn. Follow the waymarked path across two fields to another lane, cross this and another stile onto an established path across a large field into a small copse (waymarked). Once over a small footbridge, carry straight on along a track before turning left in the corner of the field, across a dyke and a footbridge over a stream. Keep following yellow arrows to cross the stile ahead, then bear right, shortly to take the path in front of a barn to the lane. Turn right,and then take the waymarked path on the left by an oast house, and follow it across fields and stiles towards Frittenden church to join a road by a hall, Turn right for the return to the church.

# Hemsted Forest to Benenden

~ Approximately 5 miles ~

*An interesting walk through pastureland and some wooded areas with streams. Lovely views of typical Kentish countryside and houses.*

**Parking**

OS Map 188 RefTQ8134. The Forestry Commission car park - Hemsted Forest

**Further Exploration**

Benenden School

The school was founded by three young teachers from Wycombe Abbey School in 1924 and established in the old manor house of Hemsted. It is now one of the top private girls' schools in the country and the Princess Royal was once a pupil here.

From the car park turn right along the lane to a T-junction, cross over and enter the driveway to Benenden School. Keep left along the drive at a new house and head towards the manor. Bear left onto another drive, shortly cross a stile on the right and head across a field to a stile and gate near a sports pavilion. Do not cross this stile, but turn left following the edge of the field to cross a stile in the right-hand corner. Cross a playing field, then at a tarmac drive turn right and follow it to the B2086. Here turn right before turning left through a small gate by a telegraph pole onto a wide grass track between houses. Beyond a stile and a gate, turn right to follow the edge of a field downhill through more stiles and gates, keeping a pond on your left-hand side as you descend to Stream Farm. Turn left along the farm track, pass through a gate and walk uphill along a sunken grass track towards a house. Cross a road via two stiles, then head diagonally towards the house, soon to cross a stile to its left into a paddock, Bear left and head towards the church, crossing two paddocks and stiles to join a track by the church, leading to Benenden green. Keep left of the green to the main road and turn left for the pub.

# King William IV (Shepherd Neame)

 The inn is said to date from the 16th century, having started as a chapel. The small saloon bar with low-beamed ceiling has a cosy atmosphere and a large inglenook fireplace. There are plenty of chairs and tables and a few interesting cushioned church pews. The public bar is plainly furnished and has an open fire, games and juke box. There is also a pleasant garden.

On draught: Shepherd Neame Spitfire, Master Brew, Original Porter(winter brew) and Bishops Finger, as well as Hurlimans and Steinbock lager. Food: home-made meals are good value, and the daily menu may include vegetable soup (£1.60), chilli (£4.15), chicken Wellington (£5.50), lamb in redcurrant sauce (£3.95), ploughman's (from £3.35) and treacle pudding (£1.80); times are 12-2pm (except Sun) and 7-9pm, Wed-Sat .

Telephone 0580 240636.

**Sissinghurst Castle Garden (National Trust)**
A large connoisseurs' garden created by Vita Sackville-West and her husband Sir Harold Nicolson around the remains of a Tudor mansion. Each area is planted either according to a seasonal theme or a colour scheme, for example, the White Garden or the Cottage Garden. Telephone: 0580 712850.

Turn right from the pub, pass the village green and take the lane to the left by the war memorial. Follow the lane for some distance, turning right onto a footpath beside a stream and chalet house and head uphill to where it widens out to a sunken track between hedges and trees. Remain on the track to cross a waymarked stile beside a gate on your left, then make for the left-hand corner of the field and pass through a gap in the hedge, keeping ahead to a gate and into an orchard, then keep to the right-hand side to follow a woodland path beyond another gate. Descend, bearing left at the bottom, and proceed uphill to a gate into pasture. Follow the left-hand fence to a stile, cross over and bear diagonally across a field towards two stiles and enter a copse. Keep ahead along the left-hand side of an orchard, then continue uphill to join a track to Red House Farm. Go through the farm to a road, turn left and walk through Goddards Green back to the car park.

# Hydon Heath to Hascombe

~ Approximately 6 miles ~

*A fairly easy walk,
with a few steep climbs
affording lovely views
across open country
Boots are essential as
the bridleways can be
very muddy.*

### Parking

OS Map 186 Ref SU 9740. The
National Trust car park off Salt
Lane.

### Further Exploration

**Winkworth Arboretum (NT)**
Pretty woodland area with rare
trees and shrubs, covering over
100 acres of hillside. The two
lakes are fringed with bluebells
in springtime. Fine views over
the North Downs.
Telephone: 048632 477.

Walk back to Salt Lane, turn right,
then almost immediately left
across the road onto a signed path
over a stile. Shortly, bear right with the yellow arrow,
then on converging with another path, turn right with
the blue arrow. At a fork, bear left, soon to climb steeply
uphill. Remain on this path, with a field to your right,
and eventually pass some houses to a lane. Keep ahead
up the lane to a junction and turn right into a no-
through road. At a fork in the road, bear left to follow the
sign for High Winkworth, then at a junction by a house
called High Hascombe, turn right onto a path along the
brick wall. The path soon widens into a narrow track,
descending steeply to a driveway. Continue down past a
couple of houses to a road. Cross over, pass through a
gate and proceed along the bridleway between two
paddocks. Bear right, pass a house called The Stables, go
through its driveway gate and keep straight ahead, soon
to reach a stile and sign on your left. Cross this and head
diagonally right to another stile, then up to another near
a shed and a gate. Continue to a road by a house. Turn
right, shortly to pass the village pond and the church to
reach the pub.

# White Horse (Friary Meux)

 Inside this attractive pub, the low beamed ceilings are hung with bunches of dried flowers and manuscripts and hunting prints adorn the walls. The carpeted lounge bar is informal and relaxing, and the separate dining area is more formally arranged. A public bar, a conservatory-style extension and a large garden with plenty of well-spaced benches complete the picture. Children are welcome away from the bar areas.

On draught: Friary Meux Best, Burton Ale, Wadworth, Guinness, Skol, Castlemaine XXXX, Lowenbrau and Strongbow cider. Food: an extensive menu may offer lamb cutlets with jacket potato (£6.95), garlic mushrooms with French bread (£1.50), cottage pie (£4.50), fresh salads (from £5.25) and a choice of home-made puddings; times are 12-2pm and 7-10pm.

Telephone: 0486 32258

On leaving the pub take the footpath directly opposite. Cross the stile and the field to another stile, then head up to another stile before a tract of woodland. At the fork in the path turn left, then right at the next fork and follow the path up to the top. Ignore the blue arrow pointing right, instead, keep straight on through the wood. At the end of this long, straight path, turn right, then immediately left and continue to the end of the path. Turn right and follow the winding path to a junction. Turn left downhill, past the gate across the path and down to a road. Cross the road diagonally to your right to a waymarked bridleway. Take the left track and climb steeply uphill. At the top, continue along the left side of a field, through a gateway and along the left side of another field before going back down into woodland. The meandering path eventually converges with another path, where you bear right uphill. Skirt the edge of a field towards some buildings and join a lane. Turn right and keep straight ahead as it turns into a muddy track, disregarding other marked paths. At a junction of paths beyond the Thames Water booster station, turn right, the path eventually taking you round one side of Hydon Hill and back to the car park.

# Thursley to Elstead

∽ Approximately 6½ miles ∽

*A pleasant meandering walk over common and heath, bog and woodland taking in part of a Nature Reserve. The OS Landranger, map is essential, as many paths criss-cross the route*

**Parking**

OS Map 186 Ref SU9040
On grass car park by cricket pitch and children's playground.

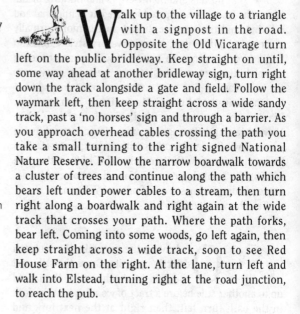

**W**alk up to the village to a triangle with a signpost in the road. Opposite the Old Vicarage turn left on the public bridleway. Keep straight on until, some way ahead at another bridleway sign, turn right down the track alongside a gate and field. Follow the waymark left, then keep straight across a wide sandy track, past a 'no horses' sign and through a barrier. As you approach overhead cables crossing the path you take a small turning to the right signed National Nature Reserve. Follow the narrow boardwalk towards a cluster of trees and continue along the path which bears left under power cables to a stream, then turn right along a boardwalk and right again at the wide track that crosses your path. Where the path forks, bear left. Coming into some woods, go left again, then keep straight across a wide track, soon to see Red House Farm on the right. At the lane, turn left and walk into Elstead, turning right at the road junction, to reach the pub.

## Woolpack (Friary Meux)

This large, low-ceilinged pub has two main rooms and a family room where children are welcome. The bars are attractive, and the atmosphere is friendly and cosy in winter when the fire is lit.

On draught: Greene King IPA and Burton. Food: a blackboard menu lists a wide range of hot and cold food and there are appetising covered displays of salads and puddings. Dishes range from jacket potatoes with different fillings (£3) and salads (around £5.50), to hot meals like beef and Guinness casserole and pork steaks with thyme, schnapps and apricot sauce (both £6.50). Puddings may include crème brûlée and chocolate and fruit scrunch; times are 12-2pm, 7-10.45pm (Sun 7.30-9pm).

Telephone: 0252 703106

**W**alk back through the village and turn left at Stacey's Farm road where a footpath sign points up beside a house. Walk uphill to the stile, cross and follow the path across the field to another stile. Cross, turn left and follow the narrow path right, away from the village and keeping the field to the left. Over the next stile, skirt the right-hand side of the field to cross another stile and carry straight on with Red House Farm on your right. Over the next stile by the gate, walk straight on towards two gates. Make for the one in the middle of the field, cross the stile and walk down the narrow path along the right-hand side of this field, over the stile straight ahead of you (ignoring the one to the right) into the woods and keep straight on where paths cross. When your path converges with another, bear left. Keep straight on over two path junctions down a long, wide bridleway until you reach a National Nature Reserve Map (No 6) on a post (take care - the post may be wrongly numbered, but the map is No 6). Turn right and continue along a wide sandy track. Where a blue waymark points left through two wooden barriers, take the very narrow path into the heather, and turn right at a track. At a 'no horses' sign, turn left down a narrow track and continue to a wooden barrier on your right where you join a track and turn left towards Thursley. Where another track crosses yours at the top, turn left, then right at a fork down the wide track towards the car park.

# Maidensgrove Scrubs to Upper Maidensgrove

〜 Approximately 4½ miles 〜

*A quiet, undulating walk through beech woods and across farmland with pleasant Chiltern views.*

**Parking**

OS Map 175 Ref SU7287. Warburg Nature Reserve car park

Turn left out of the car park, then right past Pages Farm and follow the arrowed track through beech woods to reach a house and a junction of tracks. Turn right on to the path signposted to Russell's Water and walk past a new house on the left, through a gate, and across a field to a stile on the right. Follow the white arrows down the first field, keeping to the right, then head diagonally (but avoid going too far to the right) down the next field to a stile fence and junction of paths. Go straight ahead (orange marker with green arrow) along the established track. Emerging from a small beech copse, cross the stile on the right (arrowed) and continue uphill. Cross three stiles on the left at the top of the field before crossing another field to a quiet lane. Turn right and you will soon reach the pub.

# Five Horseshoes (Brakspear)

This very popular country pub is set high up on a common among beech woods, with fine views across the Chilterns from the large, peaceful garden, and conservatory. It is a beautiful, creeper-clad cottage of brick and flint whose two neat, comfortable bars have large inglenook fireplaces, low ceilings, and wheelback chairs around wooden tables. The lounge bar walls and ceiling display an impressive collection of the world's banknotes . No children under 14 permitted in the bar.

On draught: Pale Ale, Special, Guinness, Heineken, Stella Artois. Food: the large menu includes dishes like Stilton soup (£2.50), smoked chicken pancake (£5.25), ploughman's (from £3.30), seafood tagliatelle (£6.25), and vegetarian specials. Puddings may include crème brûlée and banoffi pie (£1.95); times are 12-2pm (1.30pm Sun) and 7-10pm (9.30pm Mon, Fri and Sat). No bar food available on Sun evening.

Telephone: 0491 641282.

Turn left out of the pub and follow the quiet lane into Russell's Water. Passing the pond, bear right along the track near the Beehive pub and follow the sign to Pishill with Stonor. Pass round the back of Upper Nuttall farmhouse, through the farmyard, and follow the arrowed path through the edge of the wood. At a junction of paths, bear right and continue around the edge of the field (path PS20) to a wood. Follow the white arrows on trees through beech woods and scrubland, then cross the stile at the top of the hill and pass between two fenced paddocks towards Maidensgrove Farm. Cross the driveway to a gate and a track beside Maidensgrove Common. Cross the lane to an arrowed footpath through Maidensgrove. At end of the hamlet, near a farm, take the track ahead, climb the stile on the right and follow the waymarked footpath downhill through woodland and part of Warburg Nature Reserve, back to Pages Farm, with the car park on the right.

# Henley to Bix

~ Approximately 6 miles ~

*A pleasant undulating ramble across parkland and farmland and through woodland on the edge of the Thames Valley.*

**Parking**

OS Map 175 SU 7682. Henley town centre

**Further Exploration**

Stonor House and Park

This fine house with a Tudor façade dates back to 1190 and has been occupied by the Stonor family for 800 years. There is a medieval chapel and the treasures in the house include rare furniture, paintings, sculpture and tapestries from Britain, Europe and America. The house is set in beautiful gardens and a deer park.
Telephone: 0491 638587.

Greys Court (NT)

The gabled house dates back to the 16th century and is set amid the remains of the courtyard walls and towers of a 14th-century fortified house. The gardens includes a white garden, a rose garden  and the Archbishop's Maze, a modern pattern maze.
Telephone: (04917) 529.

From the Town Hall walk to the bottom of the Market Place and turn left onto Bell Street. At the roundabout take the A423 Oxford road, then just past the Old White Horse, turn right onto a footpath and follow it uphill into woodland. Take the path that veers left and soon reach a kissing gate. Continue ahead, over the hill to another kissing gate, beyond which you follow the track between two pig fields. Pass through a gate and follow the drive ahead, signposted Henley Park. The drive becomes unmetalled before reaching a lane. Go over the lane and stile ahead, then head diagonally right on an ill-defined path across three fields, with Middle Assendon coming into view from the last field. Head downhill to a lane. Turn left, then first right, cut across a little green and cross the B-road to a waymarked footpath. Climb uphill over four stiles to a lane and turn left uphill. Almost at the top where the lane veers sharp right, take the signed path across fields towards Bix. Pass the church and telephone box, then head down an alleyway, turning right at the end for the pub, which lies at the end of the village.

From the pub turn left along the lane to a footpath fingerpost, signed Broadplat. Cross the busy A423 and follow the lane past Bix Manor. Remain on the lane to a wood and a sharp right-hand bend. Keep ahead onto a footpath and follow the yellow arrows on trees through the wood, disregarding all other paths. Eventually emerge out onto a golf course. Proceed ahead, keeping to the left of a line of trees to a stile and a track on the far side of the course. Follow the track to where it veers sharp right and take the signed footpath left. Soon turn right along the residential Crisp Road and turn right into Hop Gardens. On reaching West Street, turn left back to the Market Place and Town Hall.

# Fox (Brakspear)

This creeper-clad brick-and-tile-built pub stood on the other side of the road until 1935 when it was flattened to make way for a new road and rebuilt by Brakspear in traditional style with lattice windows, solid oak doors and wood-panelled bars with real fires in splendid red-brick hearths. There is a cosy, welcoming, L-shaped lounge bar and a more simply furnished public bar with a fruit machine and a dartboard.

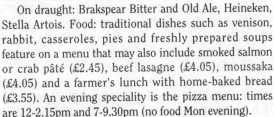

On draught: Brakspear Bitter and Old Ale, Heineken, Stella Artois. Food: traditional dishes such as venison, rabbit, casseroles, pies and freshly prepared soups feature on a menu that may also include smoked salmon or crab pâté (£2.45), beef lasagne (£4.05), moussaka (£4.05) and a farmer's lunch with home-baked bread (£3.55). An evening speciality is the pizza menu: times are 12-2.15pm and 7-9.30pm (no food Mon evening).

Telephone: 0491 574134.

# Ayot St Peter to Ayot St Lawrence

~ Approximately 5½ miles ~

*A pleasant walk through fields and woods near the home of the playwright George Bernard Shaw*

**Parking**

OS Map 166 Ref TL1916 Outside the church of Ayot St Peter.

**Further Exploration**

Shaw's Corner (NT)

This was the home of George Bernard Shaw from 1906 until his death in 1950. There are many literary and personal relics in the downstairs rooms, which remain as in his lifetime. Telephone: (0438) 820307.

**Church of Ayot St Peter**

This very attractive church has an unusual rotunda, and a beautifully ornate clockface up on the spire. The brickwork is Tudor in style, although the church is dated 1875, the original building having been destroyed by lightning the previous year.

Take the path directly opposite the church, and follow this, passing a horse paddock on your left, between woods and a field, until you reach a gate at the road, on your right. Turn left at the edge of the field, not onto the road, and aim down to the bottom corner and some woods. At a fork, bear right and on reachingt a road, turn right again. At a bend in the road, go through the gate on the left and follow the farm track to Linces Farm. As you reach the farm, follow the signposted footpath to the left, opposite a horse paddock, down towards a gap in the trees straight ahead. Follow the yellow arrows through this gap, turn left and walk along the side of the field, keeping straight and heading uphill as far as a hedge. Turn left here (not signposted), head towards Ryefield Farm, and follow the drive to the road, where you turn left. Soon after you pass the end of the wood on your left, turn right onto a bridleway which seems to cross over the road. Keep straight through the fields, on towards some buildings and a road. Turn right and signs will point you to Shaw's Corner, but before you reach it, you will see the pub on your left.

Turn left out of the pub, pass an old ruined church, and come to a junction - Shaw's Corner. Keep straight on, past the first bend in the road and footpath on the right, to the next bend, and a path on the left. Follow this to the end of the field on your right, where there is a small footpath bearing right into some woods. If the bridleway is slippery, follow this through the wood and then out to rejoin the bridleway, heading downhill to a road. Cross the road, bearing slightly left, and the bridleway continues through more fields and woods straight to a bridge. Climb the steps to the right-hand side of the bridge and turn left to go over it, and follow the disused railway line as far as the road. Turn left here and keep on this road back to your car.

## Brocket Arms (Free House)

There is a very cheerful atmosphere in this pub. Walkers are welcome, and there is a lobby in which you can leave muddy boots and other walking gear. Inside, there are old beams and inglenook fires, while outside there is plenty of seating in the attractive gardens. Children are welcome. Overnight accommodation is available.

On draught: Greene King Abbot and IPA, Wadworth 6X, Marston's Pedigree, Bass, Heineken, Kronenbourg 1664. Food: A full menu is available in the separate dining room, but usual bar meals include a cold buffet (from £3); times are 12-2.30pm and 7.30-9.30pm.

Telephone: 0438 820250.

# Cold Christmas to Wareside

~ Approximately 4 miles ~

*An easy, fairly level walk across typical Hertfordshire farmland. Stout boots or wellingtons are essential in winter as it can be very muddy.*

**Parking**

OS Map 165 Ref TL3817. Wherever the road is wide enough and it is safe.

The walk begins by a post box, where there is a telephone box to your right a few yards further down the road on a bend. Go through the white gates by the postbox, down the driveway signed as a public bridleway. As you reach the farm buildings, bear right with the track and keep on this wide, winding track, eventually reaching a road. Cross this and the stile opposite, and continue straight on past the tennis court, to another stile in the far right-hand corner. Over this, turn left down the track past a field to your left until you reach a field directly ahead. Turn right and walk around it to the opposite stile. Over this, turn left to walk through a gap in the hedge, then right towards some buildings and around the edge of the field down to a stile. Cross this, climb down the steep bank to the road, turn right, and soon turn left down a signposted track (two bollards) which takes you past a white-painted house - Bourne Cottage - to a road. Turn right to the main village road and you will see the pub to your right.

# White Horse (Greene King)

This popular pub, with its friendly staff, has two separate areas: the public bar, which houses a pool table and functions also as a family and games room; and the split-level lounge, which is cosier, with huge open fires, exposed beams covered in decorative brasses, highly polished wooden tables and comfortable cushioned seating. Ornaments and pictures (some for sale) abound.

On draught: Greene King Rayments Special and Abbot, Guinness, Kronenbourg 1664, Harp, Strongbow cider. Food: the bar menu changes regularly and may include Crofter's fish pie (£3.95), vegetable dhansak (£3.75), steak and kidney pie (£3.75), and on Sundays a traditional roast lunch at £3.75. Puddings (£1.75) may include apple pie and custard, chocolate cheesecake and pecan Danish pastry; times are 12-2pm and 7-9.30pm

Telephone: 0920 462582

Retrace your steps past Bourne Cottage, up the track to the road. Turn left and then right at a fork, passing the school on your left. Stay on this lane, passing a turning to the left, then a few houses, until it eventually turns into a narrow wooded bridleway with fields on each side, continuing gently downhill to a fork, where you turn right. As you reach the end of the wood, turn off the path, taking instead a wide grassy verge to your right, leading between the wood and a field to a gap in the trees and hedges. Through this, turn left and walk up the edge of this field to a roadwhere you turn left. Follow the road for almost quarter of a mile to a signposted footpath on your right. This wide, stony path leads gradually uphill, then veers right, but you keep straight on here to go downhill to a road, where you turn right to return to the starting point.

# Whiteleaf to Little Hampden

∽ Approximately 6½ miles ∽

*A peaceful walk among the beech woods and vales of the northern Chilterns, with some steep climbs.*

**Parking**

OS Map 165 Ref SP8203 Whiteleaf Hill car park and picnic area.

Follow the Ridgeway path from the car park along the edge of the Chiltern ridge until you reach a grassy clearing on the ridge edge. Follow the path marked with a yellow arrow on the right down through beautiful beech woods, following white arrows on trees. Cross a stile and follow the path to a quiet lane. Cross, then turn right onto an arrowed track up the valley. At the first junction of three paths, follow the narrow one ahead uphill into mature beech woods and look for directional white arrows. Continue on the white-arrowed route, ignoring other paths, over two stiles close together, and on until eventually, you reach a gate opposite a farmhouse. Bear right onto a wide track and follow it down to a road across open farmland. Cross this road and follow the arrowed path round the farmhouse and uphill into some woods. The path takes you through the woods, to the edge of an arable field, where you cross a stile and keep on through more woodland down to a quiet lane, where you will find the pub on the right.

# Rising Sun (Free House)

Tucked away up a quiet lane amongst beech woods, this is a popular haunt for walkers - although muddy boots and dogs must be left outside. There are tables on a small terrace at the front, and inside there are three small bars with standard wooden chairs, tables and cushioned bench seating. Very popular for food, its main emphasis is on being a smart pub for eating out. Children are not allowed after 8pm.

On draught: Adnams, King & Barnes, Marston's Pedigree, Murphy's, Holsten Export, Addlestone cider. Food: Good, imaginative food includes daily specials in addition to standard pub fare like woodman's (£5.65) and open farmhouse sandwiches (£3.95); times are 12.30-2pm and 7-9pm. No food either on Sunday evening or all day Monday.

Telephone: 0494 488393.

**Further Exploration**
Chequers can be seen in the distance on your outward journey. Built in 1580, this fine old house was restored by Lord Lee of Fareham, who gave it to the nation in 1919 as a country residence for the Prime Minister. Its name is said to derive from a 12th-century landowner who was a Clerk of the Exchequer.

Turn right out of the pub and soon take the waymarked path on the right beside a house. Cross a field and walk down through a wood on an established path. At the end of the wood, bear left around the edge, passing near some horse jumps. On reaching a hedge, go through to the next field and continue along its edge before turning right on the footpath down to a road. Cross and continue on the path to a stile and another road, which you cross to enter Hampden estate parkland. Bear diagonally left uphill to the gatehouse and turn right along the drive towards the church. Keep straight on through the grounds, with the house on your right and modernised barns to your left. Through a gate, keep straight along the edge of a field, eventually entering woodland by way of a new wooden barrier. This path soon crosses the bridleway (more barriers), but keep following the white arrows, past a gate, and eventually to a stile and a wide muddy track. Keep onwards until, after walking along the edge of a field to the left, you reach a track and satellite dish where you turn right onto an arrowed path through more woodland. In a short distance, take the first path sharp left and join the outward route near the ridge. Bear left for the return to the car park.

# Fingest to Skirmett

∽ Approximately 4½ miles ∽

*A peaceful walk through the wooded countryside of rural Buckinghamshire, between Marlow and Henley*

**Parking:**
OS Map 175

**Further Exploration**
Stonor House and Park
Home of Lord and Lady Camoys, the house dates back to 1180. It has a medieval Catholic chapel and some of the earliest domestic architecture in the county. The buildings treasures include rare furniture, paintings, sculptures and tapistries. The house is set in beautiful gardens and has a delightful deer park. Telephone: (0491) 638587.

From the church, turn left onto the main village road. Leave the village and take the waymarked footpath on the right. Climb a stile and follow the edge of the wood round to a gate to enter the wood. At the top of the wood follow the path diagonally left across a field, then go through another gate into another stretch of the wood Follow the track, ignoring the right-hand fork, until you join a road. Proceed straight on and take the arrowed footpath right, just beyond a brick and flint house. Cross the stile at the bottom and follow the path left to a stile and a lane. Cross the lane and stile opposite and continue straight ahead down the centre of a field towards a wood. Enter the wood and bear right, eventually reaching a gate. Beyond the gate, remain on the path downhill to a lane. Turn left into Skirmett. Turn right at a hairpin bend and follow the lane to the Old Crown, which lies on the right.

## The Old Crown (Brakspear)

This unassuming white-painted village pub was once three cottages and is over 350 years old. The interior, with its wealth of old beams, inglenook fireplace, and traditional old taproom, exudes character. Paintings, plates, bottles and tools adorn the walls. The garden is a delightful example of an old English country garden and perfect for summer eating and drinking. Children under 10 are not allowed inside.

On draught: Brakspear Bitter, Special and Old Ale, Strongbow cider. Food: the cooking is first-class, and the daily menu may offer tomato and basil soup (£2.65), medallions of pork with apricots in cream sauce (£8.95), lamb cutlets in rosemary and redcurrant jelly (£9.25) and puddings like spotted dick and chocolate truffle torte; times are 12-2pm and 7-9.30pm (not Mon). The restaurant stays open until 10.30pm.

Telephone: 049163 435.

From the pub, turn left along the road, go round the 'S' bend and take the waymarked footpath on the right. Follow the white arrows on the trees as you enter the woodland. The path becomes a track as it descends to a sharp left-hand bend. Do not follow it round, but keep straight ahead with the arrow. Your path bears diagonally right across the field, then passes through a small wood (leaving a small gas plant to the left) to a road. Cross the road, two stiles, then head diagonally right across a field and join a tarmac path on the far side. Drop down into Turville and go straight across the road in the village centre onto a waymarked path. Cross a stile, turn right and head diagonally uphill across the field, climbing two more stiles before reaching a lane. Cross the lane and follow the path to where it forks. Bear right and eventually arrive at a stile and a lane. Turn left back to the church and your car.

# Old Warden to Broom

~ Approximately 6½ miles ~

*An easy and pleasant walk through level farmland.*

### Parking
OS Map 153 Ref TL1344. Old Warden church car park (voluntary contribution).

### Further Exploration
**Shuttleworth Collection, Old Warden**
In addition to the 30 working historic aeroplanes housed in 7 hangars in this classic grass aerodrome, there is a garage of motor vehicles of the era of the 1898 Panhard Levasser. Telephone: 0767 627288.

**Swiss Garden, Old Warden**
The 9 acres of this 19th-century landscape garden contain a wealth of interesting buildings, artefacts, ponds, trees and shrubs. Closed Oct to Apr.

**Royal Society for the Protection of Birds, Sandy**
The headquarters of the RSPB includes a large and mainly woodland sanctuary Telephone: 0767 680551.

Leave the car park by way of a marked footpath directly opposite the interesting small church, and walk straight ahead until you reach some steps. Follow the footpath to the road, turn left, then shortly follow the marked footpath uphill on the right. Follow this until you reach a gate, a road and a thatched cottage. Turn left and walk along the road until you reach a sharp right-hand bend. At the bend, leave the road and follow the footpath straight ahead to cross another road. Then take the footpath almost immediately opposite which takes you around the back of some farm buildings to the village of Broom. Leaving the footpath at the sign, turn left and again left at the fork, and the pub is just a short distance on the left.

On leaving the pub follow the footpath from the pub car park. At a junction of paths, turn right and continue almost to a spinney in front of you. Turn left and when you reach the road turn right. After about quarter of a mile, turn left into the driveway to Shuttleworth College Walk past a farmhouse with almost nothing but conifers in the garden, through a white gate, and take the right-hand footpath immediately before a small bridge. Follow this, then take the left-hand footpath over a small bridge and pass through a gate to the airfield, following the path on the right alongside this to the road. Turn left and follow the road for one mile - past the Shuttleworth Aerospace Museum, the Swiss Garden and the lovely grounds of Shuttleworth College - until you see a car park sign pointing right to the church and your car.

# Cock (Greene King)

This interesting and attractive pub was made up of three Victorian cottages, and has no bar counter as staff administer drinks direct from the beer cellar There is a new restaurant area seating 30, and a sheltered garden with picnic tables and parasols. Children are welcome away from the drinks serving area, and there is a play area in the garden.

On draught: IPA, Abbot and Rayments, Kronenbourg 1664, Harp and Dry Blackthorn cider. Food: Well presented, quite imaginative dishes include chicken breast filled with Stilton, with leek sauce (£6.95), steak, mushroom and Guinness pie (£4.50) and mushroom and nut fettucini and salad (£3.50). Ploughmans come with a wide choice of cheeses, and even with a mug of soup for the very hungry (£4.25). Puddings (£1.95). There is also a separate children's menu. Food is served at 12-2pm and 6.30-9pm (lunch only, Sunday and Monday).

**Wrest Park House and Gardens, Silsoe**
The early 18th-century Baroque banqueting house is set in an attractive garden with formal canals.
Telephone: 0525 60718.

# Henley to Aston

~ Approximately 5 miles ~

*A gentle riverside walk along the established Thames path, returning with good valley views.*

**Parking**

OS Map 175 SU7682. Henley town centre

From the Town Hall in the Market Place walk down Duke Street, soon to cross over into Hart Street. Continue across Henley Bridge, over the River Thames. Take the footpath on your left, just before the Henley Royal Regatta Headquarters. Remain on this peaceful riverside path past Remenham Church, the path eventually bearing round to the right (east). Pass a lock and large weir and the village of Mill End, on the opposite side of the river. The path at this point joins a track. Bear right with the track, which brings you into the village of Aston. You will find that the pub is situated on your left, in the village.

# The Flower Pot (Brakspear)

This unspoilt, red-brick village local has a rustic public bar with a real country feel in its stripped wooden floorboards, cream-painted panelling, simple cushioned benches. An impressive display of stuffed fish decorates the walls. The garden is large and very pleasantly located with rural views over the meadows towards the River Thames.

On draught: Brakspear Bitter, Special, Old Ale and Mild, Stella Artois, Heineken, Strongbow cider. Food: a daily changing blackboard menu features good home-made food with such dishes as deep-fried butterfly prawns (£4), mushroom and nut lasagne (£4), and roast pheasant with vegetables (£5); times are 12-2pm and 6.30-9pm (On Sunday from 7pm).

Telephone: 0491 574721.

From the pub turn right and follow the lane uphill. At the top turn left through a gate onto a track and follow it uphill and round to the right. Maintain your course along this track with Thames Valley views and eventually reach a stile and a lane. Turn left up the lane for a little way to a waymarked footpath on the right. Bear diagonally left across the field, following the path into woodland. Cross a stile and leave the wood to cross a field and shortly join up with another footpath to your right. Descend to a stile near the bottom and continue across the next field, following the path right through a gap in the hedge to a kissing gate and lane. Turn left up the lane, then at the top turn right, back along road to the Thames bridge and Henley town centre.

**Further Exploration**

Henley Royal Regatta, held each year at the beginning of July, has made this pleasant Thames-side town internationally famous since late Victorian days. Over 300 of the buildings here are 'listed'. Particularly interesting is the Chantry House, which dates back to the 15th century, and numerous other historic buildings line the streets, including the Kenton Theatre, built in 1805 and the fourth oldest in England, and the attractive headquarters of Brakspear's brewery.

**Greys Court (NT)**

This charming gabled house has a 16th-century core and is set amid the remains of the courtyard walls and towers of a 14th-century fortified house. The gardens include a white garden, a rose garden and a modern 'pattern' maze, the Archbishop's Maze.
Telephone: 04917 529.

# Hungerford to Kintbury

～ Approximately 5 miles ～

*A pleasant and easy walk through the lovely Kennet Valley; the first half is along the towpath of the Kennet and Avon canal, the return across farm and common land.*

**Parking**

OS Map 174 Ref SU3468. On the town edge of Hungerford Common, by the cattle grid and the Down Gate pub.

**Further exploration**

**Hungerford**

This is a very attractive old town with a wide main street and lots of antiques and other interesting shops a pleasant place to browse around.

**Elcot**

A little way north of Kintbury, on the other side of the A4, the gardens of the Elcot Park Resort Hotel are open to the public throughout the year, free of charge. This is also a major hot-air ballooning centre and the skies around here are often full of balloons of all shapes, sizes and colours.

**T**ake the road leading off the common and into the town centre. At the end, turn right into the High Street, pass under the railway bridge and at the canal bridge, take the footpath on the right to reach the towpath. Turn right and follow this until you reach Kintbury, crossing to the other side of the canal at the first road bridge. The canal, the river Kennet and the main line from Paddington to the west, run parallel here, with the old Bath road (A4) close by. At Kintbury, cross the road bridge by the station to reach this canal-side pub.

## Dundas Arms (Free House)

Dundas is the family name of the Earls of Craven, the local nobility. The charming, unspoilt pub that bears their name has a lovely situation, bordered by the canal on two sides. On a fine day, it is worth arriving early to get a table beside the water: you may also see passengers boarding a colourful narrow boat for an afternoon trip to Newbury. Inside, there is one good-sized bar with old, dark-wood furniture, and prints and plates on the walls. The separate restaurant has a high reputation. Well-behaved children are welcome, but no dogs when food is served.

On draught: Morland Original, Charles Wells Bombardier, Eldridge Pope Hardy County, Guinness. Food: excellent bar meals include crab au gratin (£3.80),gravlax (£6.50), steak and kidney pie (£5.95), leek and gruyère pie (£5.50), smoked salmon quiche with salad (£4), and ploughman's (£4.20). If you still have room, try the chocolate brandy cake or summer pudding; times are 12-2pm, 7-9.15pm.

Telephone: 0488 58263.

Turn left out of the car park, cross the bridge and follow the road through the village of Kintbury. Take care on the section without pavement: it is quite busy and very narrow. At the end of the village, fork left towards Templeton and Inglewood Health Hydro. Continue along this delightful country lane, passing through two pairs of impressive gateways; the second marks the entrance to Inglewood Health Hydro, where the rich and famous retreat to be pampered. Ignore the bridleway opposite; the footpath you need is clearly signposted a little further along on the right. Take the path straight across the field to a little brick bridge over a drainage ditch. Here you need to keep straight, but follow the edge of the field a short way to the right. Beside a small group of trees, the path continues between two hedges, eventually bending round to the right. Do not turn with the path, but keep straight along the edge of the next field. At the end, cross a farm track and continue along the edge of another field. At the far end, cross the stile onto Hungerford Common. Keep straight across the common until you reach the intersection of the common roads. Follow the road to the left - you will see the edge of Hungerford at the far end - and this will bring you back to the cattle grid and the Down Gate pub.

**Great Bedwyn**
To the west of Hungerford, this village has a small but fascinating museum of stones, explaining the secrets of the stonemason's craft and the language of the carvings.

Further west again are the Crofton Beam Engines, one of which is the oldest working steam engine in the world (1812). For details of steam weekends, telephone: (0672) 870300. Narrow boat trips are also available here.
Telephone: 081-290 0031.

# Streatley to Aldworth

∽ Approximately 4½ miles ∽

*A gentle walk with splendid views of the Thames Valley and open downland.*

**Parking**

OS Map 174 Ref SU5980

On the A417, there is a turning (on your left if coming from Streatley) onto a road leading past the golf course and ending in the Ridgeway long-distance path. Follow the road to Warren Farm where there is a good parking area just where the Ridgeway becomes a bridleway..

**Further Exploration**

Aldworth Church

Take the lane down from the pub past the old-fashioned Post Office shop to the church which is famous for its remarkable monuments of the de la Beche family. There are nine effigies, thought to date from the 14th century, and they are so large that they are locally called the Aldworth Giants.

The village well opposite the Bell was dug in 1868 after a typhus outbreak to provide clean water and is 365ft deep.

From Warren Farm walk up the Ridgeway bridlepath which heads quite steeply uphill to your right. After the uphill stretch, you will see, ahead on your right, a short expanse of woodland, Ham Wood. Past the edge of this, take the well-defined farm track leading off almost at a right-angle on your left, going downhill, then briefly uphill, to join Ambury Lane. Turn left into the lane and walk down into Aldworth. Where the road forks, keep left for the pub.

## Bell (Free House)

This delightful inn is a long, low building with plenty of seating in the pretty garden to one side. The bars are low-ceilinged and beamed, and the main room has a vast inglenook fireplace. Mementoes of the village cricket team adorn the walls.

On draught: Hall & Woodhouse Badger Best, Hook Norton Bitter, Morrells Mild, Arkell BBB and Kingsdown. Food: bar snacks consist of a wide range of filled rolls which are excellent quality and value (from 80p to £1.50); times are 11-3pm and 6-11pm. Closed Mon (except Bank Hols).

Telephone: 0635 578272.

Turn left out of the pub and follow the lane to a T-junction with the B4009. Turn left and follow the road through Hungerford Green to Westridge Green, pass a manor house on your right, then take the footpath to the left beside a farm. The path leads through level farmland, then steeply downhill through woods to emerge into an open downland valley, crossing the bottom of a field with steeply sloping sides. At the edge of the field you meet a band of trees and join a track on your left leading back to the Ridgeway lane at Thurle Grange Farm. Turn left to return to Warren Farm.

# Oxford to Godstow

∾ Approximately 5 miles ∾

Take the A420 westwards out of the town, and pass the railway station on your right. At the river bridge, turn right onto the path on the nearside bank and follow the river north. Cross the Oxford Canal by bridge and continue along the riverbank. The next small bridge carries the path onto Fiddler's Island, at the end of which, cross the river to the opposite bank and Bossoms Boatyard. Continue along this bank to Binsey. From here, there are wide expanses of grass by the river, popular with picnicking families and paddling children; it was along this stretch of river that Lewis Carroll first told the story of Alice in Wonderland to the young Alice Liddell. Pass through the gates at Godstow Lock, and you will have the extensive ruins of Godstow Nunnery on your left. Go through the gate and turn right to cross the ancient bridge to the pub.

For the return walk, simply retrace your steps the way you came.

*This is a very easy walk, with a well defined and level path following the banks of the river.*

**Parking**

OS Map 156 Ref SP5006 (for start of walk). Park in Oxford town centre, or the 'Park and Ride' on the edge of the town. Roadside parking will be difficult near the start of the walk as it is mainly restricted to resident permit-holders. Parking at the railway station is quite expensive, but is directly on the walk route.

## Trout Inn (Bass)

Dating from the 12th century, this lovely old inn, originally the guest house for the nearby Benedictine nunnery, has certainly adapted well to today's customers and it gets really busy in summer. There are chairs and tables all along the river bank outside the inn, and an exotic touch is provided by the peacocks that roam about between the tables. Although the riverside is so popular, the inn retains its ancient character inside and children and dogs (on a lead) are welcome.

On draught: Bass, Worthington, Guinness, Tennents, Carling Black Label and Dry Blackthorn cider. Food: there is a snack bar serving various dishes, for example, lasagne, curry, salads and ploughman's, at prices ranging from £1.80 to £5.60, and there is also a restaurant offering a full menu; times are 12-2.30pm, 6-10pm, or all day in summer.

Telephone: 0865 54485.

# Sandford St Martin to Great Tew

~ Approximately 6½ miles ~

*A delightful walk through undulating North Oxfordshire countryside and through idyllic honey-coloured stone villages.*

**Parking**
OS Map 164 Ref SP4226
Sandford St Martin Church.

Head north out of the village and in quarter of a mile, take a track off to the right (by a yellow hydrant) towards some thatched cottages. Pass in front of the cottages and bear left, following the path through a gate and across the field, keeping to the wall on the left. Pass through a gate and follow the path beside some houses onto a lane. Bear left to the crossroads where you keep straight until you reach a turning on the right leading to Hobbs Hole Farm. Pass behind the farm and bear left onto a track, keeping to the left-hand edge of the fields. You will eventually follow the wall of Great Tew Park on the left before passing through two gates, and following a lane past some beautiful thatched cottages, into the village, with the pub immediately to the right.

Bear right in front of the row of stone-built thatched cottages, and cross the small green on the left beside the school, passing through a kissing gate over the quiet lane. Bear diagonally left uphill across a field and pass behind the farm. Through a gate, cross a field, keeping to the right-hand edge, to a kissing gate and a road. Cross the next field diagonally, keeping the radio-mast to the left. At the corner of the field, join a lane and bear right into Little Tew. Take the waymarked path beside the first house on the left, cross a stile and head for another stile in the hedge ahead. Bear diagonally right across the field towards a farm and join a road. Turn right and soon cross a small brook and turn left along the track beside it. Pass through a gate towards a derelict house, soon bearing right through another gate. Keep to the footpath along the right-hand edge of the field and eventually join a lane near Tracy Farm. Turn left and follow this lane, keeping left towards woodland, then turn right towards Beaconsfield Farm. Pass the farm and keep straight on, then take the track on the right and follow this to the lane, where you turn right back to Sandford St Martin church.

# Falkland Arms (Free House)

A feeling of timelessness prevails in this partly thatched, wisteria-covered building. Within the old stone walls, the bar has a superb inglenook fireplace, stone-flagged floors, high-backed settles, oak panels and beams, and a ceiling bedecked with a collection of old beer and cider mugs. The tiny bar claims to dispense more different traditional ales in a year than any other pub in Britain. You can also buy clay pipes, tobacco and snuff here. Outside, there is a front terrace with tables and chairs, and a garden at the back with more seating where geese and ducks wander. Children are welcome in the eating area.

On draught: Donnington Best, Hook Norton Best, Wadworth 6X, Tuborg, Hall & Woodhouse Tanglefoot, Guinness and regularly changing guest ales. Food: traditional bar food is served in generous portions. A changing blackboard menu includes pork and Stilton pie (£5), cheese and lentil loaf (£4.50), chicken in cider (£5) and home-made puddings (£1.60); times are 12-2pm (not Sun or Mon lunchtime).

Telephone: 060883 653.

# Fifield to Shipton-under-Wychwood

∽ Approximately 6½ miles ∽

*A long but gentle walk on the eastern fringe of the Cotswolds, traversing woodland and open fields. Can be very wet and muddy after prolonged periods of rain.*

**Parking:**

OS Map 163 Ref SP2418 On the minor road beside Fifield church

Go through the churchyard then turn right onto the village road. Where the road bends right, carry on down the track and through the gate into Fifield Common. Follow the path for about three-quarters of a mile to reach a gate and woods. Shortly, take the right fork (D'Arcy Dalton Way). Do not go on the track but follow the right-hand edge of the field, soon to rejoin the track and continue ahead at the crossways up the slope. Follow the zig-zag track for quarter of a mile to where it bends right over a cattle grid towards farm buildings. Continue ahead with the hedge on your right to a lane where you turn right and left at the T-junction. On approaching Bruern Abbey School, bear right onto the waymarked 'Oxfordshire Way', walk through the grounds and into Bruern Wood. At the end of the wide clearing, go through the gate and follow the hedge on the right. Maintain this direction along the defined path to the outskirts of Shipton. Go left down by a hedge and turn right onto Meadow Lane, which leads to the A361. Turn right and walk through the village to the Shaven Crown. (There is another very pleasant inn here, the Lamb, owned and run by an Italian family, and this, although not so spectacular a setting, would also be a good place to stop).

# Shaven Crown (Free House)

This magnificent Cotswold-stone inn was formerly a guest house for Bruern Abbey, before becoming an inn 600 years ago. A medieval flagstoned archway leads through to a delightful cobbled courtyard with tables and chairs around a central fish pond. Inside, the bar has high-beamed ceilings, padded settles arranged in alcoves and a large stone fireplace. What was the medieval Great Hall is now the reception area. There are nine bedrooms. Children are welcome, but no dogs.

On draught: Hook Norton Best Bitter, Bentleys Yorkshire Bitter, a guest ale, Murphy's, Lowenbrau and Blands Blackjack Cider. Food: on the menu you may find soup (£1.75), smoked haddock (£2.95), mushroom and spinach pancake (£2.95), spinach and bacon lasagne (£4.95), sirloin steak (£7.95), pigeon salad vinaigrette (£2.95). Desserts cost around £1.85; times are 12-2pm, 7-9.30pm (Sun 9pm). Telephone: 0993 830330.

**Further Exploration**

The 'Wychwood' villages get their name from Wychwood Forest, the medieval hunting ground that once covered much of West Oxfordshire. The remnants of the ancient woodland are two miles east of Shipton on the west slopes of the Evenlode Valley. Shipton-under-Wychwood contains many fine stone buildings, including Shipton Court, one of the largest Jacobean houses in England (not open to public).

From the Shaven Crown go right along the A361. At the sharp left-hand bend take the track ahead signed 'Milton-under-Wychwood'. Where it opens into a pasture by a kissing gate, bear slightly right, follow the boundary down to cross a stream. Proceed across two fields towards the left of a row of houses to emerge into Jubilee Lane and continue to the High Street. Turn right, then after 50 yards take the path left. Proceed across the fields, then continue along the track to Grange Farm and the road. Turn left and, after the cottages, take a waymarked path right. Cross the field diagonally left to a stile, then bear right along the hedge (trees to the right) to the next stile. Follow the stream and at a concrete bridge bear left to a stile. Follow the path diagonally over the fields towards Fifield. Bear left past the playground to the road. Turn left, and bear round to the right back to the church.

# Gloucester Beeches to Cockleford

~ Approximately 4 miles ~

*A delightful walk in the heart of Roman Gloucestershire. Starting from the Ermin Way, the route incorporates the wooded flanks of the Churn valley, Cowley Park and the interesting village of Elkstone.*

**Parking**

OS Map 163 Ref SO9512
Gloucester Beeches Lay-by on the A417.

**Further Exploration**

Devil's Chimney on Leckhampton Hill, north-east of Cockleford, is a 50ft pinnacle of limestone, rising out of a quarried area. There are magnificent views over the Vale of Gloucester.

**Chedworth Roman Villa**

Some of the finest remains of any Roman villa in Britain can be seen here. Mosaics and two bath houses are well preserved. Telephone: 0242 890256.

**W**alk north-westwards down the lay-by, passing the toilets, then go up the steps in the right-hand bank. Cross the busy A417 and enter the lane opposite. Immediately, go through the left-hand gate and head across the field to a stone wall. With the wall to your left shortly emerge onto a lane and keep ahead to a T-junction. Take the waymarked path across the field opposite, looking for a gate on the edge of woodland. Walk down a wide clearing, past a wooden hut on your left, over a forest track and down the steep grassy path, known as The View. Remain on the woodland path and eventually merge with a forest track, following it round a left, then a right-hand bend to where it bears left again. Take the narrow path right, up the steep wooded bank to a stile. Cross and follow the path to the left of a line of trees, up the field to a road and turn right. Climb the next stile on the right following the waymarked path diagonally down to another lane. Turn right and follow the lane to the pub.

## Green Dragon (Free House)

This lovely old pub, clad in vine and wisteria, occupies a peaceful position looking up the Churn valley. Heavy studded doors lead to a choice of three bars all with an old-world rustic ambience. Low-beamed ceilings, exposed stone walls, a mix of bare wooden floorboards, flagstones and carpets, open fires and woodburners and an array of comfortable furniture help make this a cosy pub in which to relax. There is good outdoor seating, specially on the terrace overlooking the lake. Children welcome.At the time of our visit the following refreshments were typical of the pub, but as we went to press we heard that the pub might change hands.

On draught: a choice of at least six real ales - Hook Norton Best, Bass, Greene King Abbot Ale, Wadworth 6X, Theakstons Old Peculier, Smiles Exhibition, Murphy's, Guinness, Newquay Steam pils, Stella Artois, and Strongbow and Bulmers ciders. Food: the menu may

include peppered mushrooms (£1.75), garlic snails (£2.50), chicken Marengo (£4.75), and whiskied pheasant (£6). Lighter bites include ploughman's (from £3), salmon quiche (£4) and cold roast beef (£3.25); times are 11.15am-2pm, 6.15-10pm, (Sun 12-2.30pm, 7.15-10pm).

Telephone: 0242 870271.

From the pub turn left uphill and shortly turn left to follow a lane for half a mile. Opposite Millstone Cottage take the waymarked path on the right. Do not go up the track, but, turn back on yourself and go round the right-hand edge of a field to cross a wooden bridge over a stream. Turn left up a narrow woodland path to a gate. Here the path becomes ill-defined as you bear half-left searching for the yellow arrows on the trees. Head across a series of hummocks, then over steep, rough terrain to a gate and a road. Turn right, then left over a stile and head across a field towards the tree in the right-hand hedge. Follow the hedge to a wall, bear left round a cottage, over a stile, then up the side of the cottage to another stile and into the village of Elkstone. Turn right by the chapel onto the village street, then turn left down a gravel road and take the right fork to a white gate. Bear left along the footpath, keeping to the left-hand side of a paddock and a field, and head for the church. Turn right onto the church drive, then left at the road to reach a crossroads. Turn right, then at the bottom of the hill take the waymarked route left along a track, then up the field to a stile in the hedge. Bear slightly right to the hedge on the right and follow it to the A417 and the lay-by.

**Coberley Church**

Interesting stone effigies are worth a visit, including one of Sir Thomas Berkeley who fought at Crecy and died around 1350, and his wife Joan who took as her second husband Sir William Whittington and gave birth to Richard, reputedly the Dick Whittington of pantomime fame.

**Elkstone Church**

One of the most interesting churches in the area, dating from 1160 and having many Saxon and Norman features.

# Stanton to Snowshill

⌘ Approximately 6½ miles ⌘

*This is a classic walk along the Cotswolds ridge with panoramic views across the Vale of Evesham, taking in three of the most picturesque Cotswold-stone villages.*

**Parking**

OS Map 150 Ref SP0634. Car park on edge of Stanton village.

Turn right onto a lane and enter the charming village of Stanton with its manyt cottages built of honey-coloured stone, bearing left at the first junction into the main street  Walk up to a small green, and bear right along a lane onto a track which soon becomes a footpath - the Cotswold Way. Follow the yellow arrows across two stiles near a  waterworks, then bear right for a long but rewarding climb uphill. At the top of the hill, pass through a gate near a farm and cross the field, then turn right along a track through the farmyard and around the front of the house. Bear left to a gateway, turn left then right  to go diagonally across two fields on an established path. On reaching a narrow lane, turn right and continue into Snowshill. The pub lies opposite the church and village green.

# Snowshill Arms (Donnington)

This attractive stone-built pub is beautifully situated next to the village green which is enclosed by charming old cottages. Inside, the airy open-plan beamed bar is partly panelled, with stripped stone walls visible in places. Simple furnishings include comfortable wall-benches, pine tables and seats on a carpeted floor. Some prints and local photographs adorn the walls. Good seating is available in the garden which has a play area for children, and valley views.

On draught: Donnington Best and SBA, Guinness, Lowenbrau, Carlsberg. Food: the wide selection of bar food includes sandwiches (from £1.75), ploughman's (£2.75), salads (from £2.75) and basket meals (from £2.75); times are 12-2pm and 6.30-9.15pm.

Telephone: 0386 852653.

**R**etrace your steps along the lane until you reach Oat Hill farmhouse, where you follow the waymarked path downhill through a gate. Follow yellow arrows and posts on the footpath across fields towards a farmhouse on a hill. When you join a track, bear left then right onto another track which goes round the back of the farm. Follow it to a gateway, where you bear left across the field towards a stone gatepost. Cross the nearby stile and follow the arrowed path downhill. On reaching a stile at the bottom of hill near Buckland Manor, bear left and follow the yellow arrows across fields. Pass to the north of Laverton village, and Stanton soon comes into view. Take the arrowed path downhill towards the church and continue alongside the wall into the churchyard and eventually onto Stanton's main street. Bear right, then right at the end, back to the car park.

## Further Exploration

Stanton is the perfect Cotswold village, totally unspoilt, with its main street lined with beautiful golden-stoned houses with steeply-pitched gables, most dating from 1600. Tucked behind the village cross is St Michael's Church which is particularly notable for its furnishings by Sir Ninian Comper. Some medieval pews survive, their poppy heads gouged deep from the days when shepherds took their dogs to church and fastened them to the pew heads.

## Snowshill Manor (National Trust)

This 16th-century manor house has a terraced garden full of old-fashioned roses, shrubs and ponds. Inside is the collection amassed by Charles Wade, including English, European and Oriental furniture, craft tools, toys, clocks, bicycles and musical instruments. There is also a collection of Japanese Samurai armour. Telephone: 0386 852410.

# Moreton-in-Marsh to Blockley

~ Approximately 6 miles ~

*A fairly strenuous walk in open countryside which encompasses Batsford Park and Aboretum.*

**Parking**

OS Map 151 Ref SP205325 Town centre car park, except Tue.

**Further exploration**

The church at Blockley is well worth a visit. It was founded in AD 855 but most of the building is Norman or later.

**Batsford Arboretum**

The 50 acres of land contain one of the largest collections of trees in Great Britain, and there are many rare and beautiful species. Telephone: 0608 50722 and 0386 700409 (weekends).

**Cotswold Falconry Centre**

Situated by the Batsford Arboretum, the centre has dailyydemonstrations. Telephone: 0386 701043.

**Sezincote**

For a taste of the exotic, visit this Indian-style house which was the inspiration for the Prince Regent's Brighton Pavilion. There is also a charming water garden in the beautiful grounds.

Go down the lane beside the Co-op, straight on along a footpath, then across the middle of a common. Pass under the electric wires and after 100 yards cross the stile in the hedge on the left. Maintain the original direction across pastures for about a mile. On reaching a copse go over a tiny stone bridge and continue, keeping the copse to the right, until reaching a high stone wall and signpost. Turn right and take the path which leads you along the south-east boundary of Batsford Park to a road. Turn left, pass the Batsford turning and head straight on up the hill at the next junction. Near the top, where the road bears left, take the signed bridleway across the field. After quarter of a mile at a crossways of paths follow the blue arrows straight on along the ridge, then drop downhill onto a farm track to a road. Turn right at the main road, then take the next left up through the churchyard and out to the main village street. Turn left for the pub.

## Crown Inn (Free House)

This golden-stone Elizabethan inn is situated in the heart of the village. The bar and cosy lounge are welcoming and comfortably furnished in keeping with the surroundings and there are two restaurants. In fine weather, tables are set out on the main street and in the old coach yard. Staff are friendly and dogs, but not children, are allowed in the bar.

On draught: Hook Norton Best, Robinson's Bitter Courage Directors, Fosters, Kronenbourg 1664, Guinness, Beamish, and guest beers. Food: bar snacks range from sandwiches (from £2) and ploughmans (from £3.95) to daily specials like pork fillet and thyme sauce (£6.95), and avocado and stilton bake (£3.95). One of the two restaurants specialises in fish, delivered fresh from Cornwall three times a week. Times are 12-2.15pm and 7-10pm in the bars and fish restaurant; 7-9.30pm in the other restaurant.

Telephone: 0386 700245.

O n leaving the pub, turn left, then take the next right down a steep hill. Follow this road round to the main road, turn left and after 200 yards turn right up the footpath marked Heart of England Way. Follow it uphill past a farmhouse, and continue steeply up to a stile. Turn left in the belt of trees, go through a gate and turn right by a stone wall on the right. Cross the road into the wood, follow the stone wall on your left, passing trial jumps, then on downhill to bear right to a stony drive.Turn left on nearing a lodge, bear right over a stile and go down to cross the main drive and enter the field opposite. Follow the path by the stone wall on the left  to rejoin the outward path for the return to Moreton-in-Marsh and the car park.

# Staunton to Newland
∽ Approximately 6 miles ∽

*A strenuous walk up and down hills and valleys and along Offa's Dyke Path with excellent views of the Wye Valley and the Forest of Dean.*

**Parking**

OS Map 162 Ref SO 5312
Extended layby on the left of A4136 (as you come from Monmouth) just before a sign for Forest of Dean and before entering Buckstone.

**Further Exploration**
'The Cathedral of the Forest', Newland
The village church as it now stands was begun about 1200 and houses several chapels which in the past, would each have had their own staff of priests, quite separate from the main church and the high altar.

Walk up the side of the A4136 into Staunton. Turn right after the White Horse Inn, then left and right again, following road signs for Newland and Redbrook. Take the track to the left, fork right at the cottages and continue for about three-quarters of a mile. After a sharp turn to the left, passing pines either side and a path which transects the bridleway, go down the next track to the right. At a T-junction of tracks turn left, then after quarter of a mile cross a stile on the right and continue down the field to arrive at a road junction. Turn left and right up a marked footpath by an old railway gate and continue to the right of the fields. Cross the field at the end of the track, go over the stile and dyke, then bear right down the next field to another stile. Cross the track and then pass through to the far left corner of the field opposite. Turn right to reach the road, then left into Newland, and the pub.

Turn back to the right from the pub. As you leave the village, bear left up the marked route for Upper Redbrook bearing left across a field to a gate. Follow the yellow markers over gates and stiles until - after about a mile - the path brings you down to a road. Cross this and take the path opposite, and when it brings you to a lane continue up. Walk along this track (well marked as Offa's Dyke Path), with the Wye Valley below to the left and the fringes of the Forest of Dean to the right, until you reach an old stone barn on the left. Here cross the stile to the right, then go up to the left until a metal swing gate brings you up to a National Trust car park. Past the 'naval temple' there is an observation point down to the left over Monmouth and towards Wales. Now bear right over the downhill stile following the sign to Staunton Road and keep on down towards the distant A4136. After a stile to the left of some holly bushes, turn right and follow the track until it meets the main road. Turn right to get back to the parking area.

# Ostrich Inn (Free House)

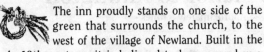

The inn proudly stands on one side of the green that surrounds the church, to the west of the village of Newland. Built in the early 13th century, it is believed to have served as a hospice to the church during its extension and reconstruction. The bar is softly lit and has a low beamed ceiling and a huge inglenook fireplace, around which is an array of wooden furniture, including some antique settles.The atmosphere is quiet and easy, as befits the village setting. There is a beer garden at the back and there are also some benches at the front overlooking the church and green.

On draught: Boddingtons, Marston's Pedigree, Shepherd Neame Spitfire, Ringwood Old Thumper, Murphy's, Dortmunder Union, Heineken, Blackthorn cider. Food: the home-made food tastes very good and comes in generous helpings: the blackboard menu is supplemented by an extra choice of lunchtime specials - for example, chicken breast in pernod and cream (£6.50), or John Dory in butter and herbs. There are also ploughman's with cheeses or Cumberland sausage (£3.95). Puddings cost around £2.50; times are 12-2pm and 7-9pm.

Telephone: 0594 833260.

# Hidcote Manor to Ilmington

~ Approximately 5 miles ~

*This walk has some steep slopes but is otherwise fairly gentle. Allow time at the end of the walk to visit Hidcote Gardens.*

**Parking**

OS Map 151 Ref SP1743 Left-hand car park at Hidcote Manor.

**W**alk through the gate at the end of the overflow car park and then diagonally across the field to your right, up towards the hedge, over the stile and over the next one immediately to the left, as signposted (yellow arrows). Follow the path straight on, then shortly bear left downhill to a gate near some pine trees. Cross the small plantation, a meadow and a wood, then drop down to the stream's edge and follow the path across several fields, under a line of pylons to a road. Turn right and right again at the T-junction, turning right yet again after Larkstone Cottage. Take the next left, then, after 50 yards, the marked footpath into a field. Go down the right-hand edge of the field to a stile on your right, cross two streams, and turn half-right uphill to a stile. Keep on uphill, with the hedge to the right. Soon after the top, bear right over a stile and go diagonally across the field, with the pond on your left. Turn left before the third stile, follow the fence, go through a gate and follow the track between two houses to the road. Go left and take the footpath right past the church, then fork left through the churchyard to some cottages. Turn left and follow the stream to a road leading to the pub.

Cross the green to the main road and turn right along the pavement, soon passing the Red Lion. At the village green, cross the road and walk along the top of the green to the far end. Take the no-through road above the thatched cottage. At the end of the road take the footpath between the hedges, ignoring the first stile on the right. Just before reaching a gate cross two stiles on the right, then turn left uphill, keeping the hedged fence on your left. Turn right along the ridge and follow the track over the hill, past the masts to a road. Go through the gate opposite and the one beyond and walk through the trees. Follow the path ahead keeping the stone wall on the right. Cross over the next lane and follow the track down to Hidcote and the car park.

## Howard Arms (Flowers)

Attractively situated overlooking a green, this pub is neatly furnished with cushioned chairs, old-fashioned settles and comfortable window seats. There are heavy beams, a huge inglenook fireplace, and rugs covering the flagstone floor. The separate restaurant is suitable for large parties at any time. Outside, the large garden is pleasant for summer dringking. Children are welcome. Two guest bedrooms are available.

On draught: Flowers Best, Marston's Pedigree and a guest ale as well as Guinness, Heineken, Stella Artois and Strongbow cider. Food: the regularly changing menu includes soup (£2), sandwiches (from £1.75), ploughman's (from £3.25), and hot dishes like deep-fried brie with redcurrants (£3.25), seafood croissant (£5.95) and lamb, leek and rosemary pie (£5). Desserts at around £2.50 may include crème brûlée or steamed treacle sponge; times are 12-2pm and 7-9pm, (not Sun evening). The restaurant is open 7-9pm, Tue-Thu (9.30pm Fri and Sat). Sunday lunch in the restaurant is £11.25.

Telephone: 0608 82226.

### Further Exploration

The church at Ilmington is worth a visit. It has examples of early Norman arches, and an early Norman bell tower. In Tudor times, the church was altered considerably with the addition of the first storey and the transepts. Above the south door is a medieval niche which would have held a statuette of the patron saint of the church.

### Hidcote Manor Garden

These formal and informal gardens, laid out by Major Lawrence Johnston over 40 years, contain many rare trees, shrubs and plants of all kinds. They now belong to the National Trust.

Telephone: 0386 438333.

# Sutton-under-Brailes to Upper Brailes
~ Approximately 5 miles ~

*This walk discovers the contrasts between the three Brailes villages, via a riverside ramble along the Sutton Brook and a hillside section with valley views.*

**Parking**
OS Map 151 Ref SP 2937. Limited parking by Sutton-under-Brailes church. Do not obstruct the entrance or park on the village green.

**Further Exploration**
The Rollright Stones
This principally Bronze-Age stone circle, known as the King's Men, lies on a ridge west of the A3400, 5 miles south of Sutton-under-Brailes and mystery surrounds its real origin and purpose, though legend has it that the king and his knights were turned to stone by a witch.

St George's Church in Lower Brailes is known as 'the Cathedral of the Feldon' and is one of the grandest churches in Warwickshire. Today, the huge church is the only reminder of the village's past importance.

**W**alk down to the village green and along the road towards Brailes. After Greenhill Farm bear right down the track and cross the river. Shortly, turn left onto the waymarked path and with the river on your left proceed across the golf course, then along the edge of fields to the outskirts of Lower Brailes. In the paddock, immediately before the village, bear half-right to a stile. Do not cross it, but bear left for the stile in the bottom corner. Go over the track and along the path over the brook, then fork right to the road, ignoring the stile. Take the lane almost opposite, past the hairdressers and Feldon House car park, then shortly, go left through a gate into a paddock and follow the left boundary down to cross the metal river bridge. Proceed up the steps opposite and keep ahead through two fields. Cross the next field and head for a stile in the hedge opposite (not the one slightly to the right). Go over the road and straight on through more paddocks, with the hedge to your right, to the main road. Turn right for the pub.

## The Gate (Hook Norton)

This homely stone-built village inn consists of a simple public bar with open fire and a welcoming lounge with low-beamed ceiling, exposed stone walls, large inglenook and an assortment of rustic furniture. There is a large lawn with barbecue and tables to the rear and a small front lawn. Children and dogs are welcome.

On draught: Hook Norton Best, Old Hookey and Mild, Guinness, Heineken, Carlsberg Export, Scrumpy Jack cider. Food: good value for money, the menu offers dishes like egg and chips (£1.50), sandwiches (from £1.25), vegetable chilli (£4.10), chicken curry (£4.10), mushroom and nut fettucini (£4.10), gammon (£3.85), ploughman's (from £3.85) and puddings like spotted dick (£1.80); times are 12-2pm and 7-9.30pm.
Telephone: 0608 85212.

From the pub go back down the road. Where it bends left, cross over and, just after the small lay-by, cross the grass and take the signed path right. Cross a paddock and a stream, then pass through an old orchard to emerge on a lane via a stile. Turn right and after quarter of a mile, by Lazy Moon Farm, take the waymarked bridleway right up a steep tree-lined cleft. At the top, go through a gate and across fields, with the hedge on your right, to the farm buildings. Pass the barns on your left and bear slightly right through a gate and follow the bridleway uphill. When the path levels out, carry on to a gate, turn left past the pine trees and head downhill. Proceed down a steep, grassy slope to a concrete drive. Continue past a stable and then look for a stile on the left. Head diagonally over the field towards the church, cross a stile into an orchard; continue past a house, then the church, and so to the road and your car.

# Eardisley to Winforton

~ Approximately 4½ miles ~

*A short walk across tracks and meadows through the scenic Wye Valley.*

**Parking**

OS Map 148 Ref SO3149. Eardisley Church

**Further Exploration**

Winforton church is named for St Cynidr, who began a hermitage on an island in the Wye in the 6th century. The church has an unusual 16th-century timber bell chamber on top of a medieval stone tower.

Follow the bridleway sign round behind the church, and remain on the metalled lane to the barn in the second large field. Go through the metal gate on the left and cross the field diagonally to the right-hand side of a clump of conifers. Go along the back of the trees to a stile in the corner. Head across the field to the black swing gate, cross the disused railway into Lady Arbour farmyard, and turn right between the farm buildings. Take the track ahead at the crossroads of tracks. Pass in front of a timbered cottage and remain on the track to a quiet lane. Turn left and follow it for a quarter of a mile to the main road. Turn right to the pub.

## The Sun (Free House)

This unassuming building houses a neatly kept bar with wood-burning stoves, high settles and a mixture of country furnishings. The exposed stone walls are studded with agricultural implements and the atmosphere is relaxed and friendly. There is a garden and a play area, and children are allowed in the bar if they are eating.

On draught: Brains, Boddingtons, Wood's Parish, Flowers Original, Weston's cider. Food: imaginative dishes on the menu may include vegetable biryani with cashew nuts (£4.99), salmon with bacon and laverbread sauce (£8.99), home-made soups (£1.50) and Welsh chicken and leek pie (£5.99). Unusual desserts (£2.95) include crème de cacao mousse and 'nuts about nuts' tart, and there is also a fine selection of English and Welsh cheeses; times are 12-2pm and 7-9.30pm (9.45pm Fri and Sat). Closed on Tuesdays from November until Easter.

Telephone: 0544 327677.

Turn right out of the pub and walk along the pavement for a short distance before turning right through a timber yard to a gate ahead. Cross to another gate, then follow the path across common land, keeping left of the small timbered cottage, to a gate. Cross a bridge and a field to an old gateway then cross the field and go uphill, with the hedge on the right to a gate and a narrow lane. Turn left and where it turns left into a driveway, bear right onto a track (can be muddy), remaining on this around the edge of the wood. Cross an old railway bridge and soon emerge from the woodland onto a lane beside a house. Climb the stile on the right just past the driveway and follow the waymarked path through two gates and fields to join an established track. Pass the farm and Eardisley Park House where the track becomes metalled, and remain on this back to the church and your car.

# Clehonger to Ruckhall

~ Approximately 5½ miles ~

*A pleasant walk above the Wye Valley close to the cathedral city of Hereford. There are spectacular views over the river from the delightful Ancient Camp Inn, once the site of an Iron Age camp.*

**Parking**

OS Map 149 Ref SO4637
Clehonger church.

From the front of the church, turn left and follow the road to a farm track on the left (footpath sign). Follow this past the farm and a group of cottages then, in a short distance, turn right. Follow the minor power line to cross the stile, and continue to a gate alongside a farm. Through this, turn left onto a minor road. When you reach an orchard on the left, turn right through a gateway. Cross the field to a gate before bearing left through another gate into a small copse. Descend and go through a gate beside a cottage, past Tuck Mill and across a small brook before turning right through another gate. Keep left around the wire perimeter fence of a sub-power station, continue straight ahead, then, in a short distance, cross a stile, ascend the steps on your left and continue along the path to the pub.

## Ancient Camp Inn (Free House)

This secluded inn derives its name from the Iron-Age hill fort on whose ramparts it stands, some 80 feet above the River Wye, offering breathtaking views along the river. Flagstone floors, open fires and wooden furniture characterise a rustic charm, while the lounge bar offers inviting sofas.People dressed for walking should note that the pub requests smart, casual dress , but there is no problem in warm weather as there is a very pretty front terrace on which walkers can enjoy a wonderful lunch and a stunning view. Well-behaved children are welcome at lunchtime only.

On draught: Wood's Parish Bitter, West Country IPA, Guinness, Heineken, Stella Artois and Strongbow cider. Food: the menu may include dishes like ham and celery au gratin (£5.25), Greek shepherd's pie with salad, cannelloni filled with Ricotta cheese and spinach (both £5.75), and ploughman's (£3.75). There is a choice of desserts at £2.75; times are 12-2pm and 7-9.30pm. Closed Mon, no bar food Sun evening.
Telephone: 0981 250449.

From the pub, turn right onto a waymarked path at the end of the car park, then turn right with the footpath sign, descend the path to the river bank and bear left along its path. Over the stile in the left-hand corner, cross a footbridge and continue along the river bank. At a junction of paths, turn left then pass through a gate and continue up a track to pass a cottage, then turn left over a stile to cross a field. Keep on this path over stiles, fields and a footbridge, heading for the distant Eaton Bishop church. At a road, turn left to Eaton Bishop, past the church then, at the telephone box, turn left on the nearside of a black and white cottage, and go across fields and two stiles, then take the left-hand fork to join the road. Just before you reach a tiny hamlet, follow the sign to the right across the field, alongside a wooded brook. At the end of the field, cross the stile and footbridge, then keep straight ahead to cross the next field on the side of a hill, away from the brook. Through the next gate, turn left and cross the brook by footbridge. Walk diagonally to the right towards an old oak tree, but staying at the foot of the hill. Cross another footbridge, then ascend the path past a small building. Cross a stile concealed in a shrub at the top of the hill, turn right to the end of the field, and over another two stiles to the main road. Turn left, proceeding with care, then at the top of an ascent, turn left along a drive (footpath sign). At the far corner of the right-hand warehouse (where the road surface ends), turn right through the gate. Cross two more fields and stiles and return to the church.

# Sollers Hope to Woolhope

∾ Approximately 6 miles ∾

*An extremely pleasant walk in quiet, wooded country high above the Wye Valley, following the line of Ridge Hill (758ft) and Marcle Hill. The return to the peaceful village of Sollers Hope is a gentler walk through farmland.*

### Parking

OS Map 149 Ref SO6133. Sollers Hope church. Space is limited, so be careful not to block the farm entrance.

Head east away from the front gate of the churchyard, cross the road and the stile opposite. Pass some farm outbuildings to the left, keep a small stream on the right then go through a gate, cross the field and through a further two gates until, alongside an old stone barn, turn left onto a narrow road. Through the gate on the right, follow the path beside the brook, head uphill to a stile, then bear left onto a lane, cross a stream, and keep left up a track to begin the long ascent of a wooded footpath. At the summit, turn left over a stile (walkers sign) and climb the steps to cross a stile and continue along Ridge Hill, following the yellow footpath arrow. Cross the next stile to pass a triangulation pillar (758ft), then cross three more stiles before, in the corner of the field, descending the steps to a road which follows Marcle Hill. Opposite Hooper's Oak Cottage, turn left and descend a footpath. Through the gate, cross a large field, following the line of the hedgerow. Over the stile in the far right-hand corner, ascend through a small copse, climb the stile at the end, cross a field, and pass through the gate to join a wooded track. Descend this track, and later the tarmac road, to reach the pub.

# Butchers Arms (Free House)

This is a distinctive black and white, half-timbered country inn, dating back to the 14th century. Welcoming log fires in winter warm its two cosy, beamed bars, while in summer, French windows give access onto a pleasant patio garden and stream. Children are welcome.

On draught: Hook Norton Best and Old Hookey, Marston's Pedigree, Carlsberg, and a different guest beer each week. Food: tasty, well presented dishes frequently on the menu may include ploughman's (£3.25), Woolhope pie, packed with rabbit and bacon and cooked in local cider (£4.95), mushroom Biryani, garnished with cucumber, tomatoes and coconut, and served with dhal (£4.95). Sweets are wonderful and extraordinary value at £1.75; try the home-made apple pie, treacle tart, or chocolate brandy refrigerator cake; times are 12-2pm and 7-10pm (Fri and Sat 10.15pm).

Telephone: 0432 860281.

Turn left out of the pub to join the main road, and continue ascending gradually into Woolhope village. Pass the church and the Crown Inn and, in a short distance, turn left over a stile. Cross fields, stiles and a footbridge over a stream, keep to the right of the willow tree and continue over more stiles, a road and two fields to a farm road. Keep walking straight until you reach a fork in the path. Go through the centre gate (painted blue), cross the field and climb the stile ahead. Follow the path round to the left, and cross the next stile up ahead over the stream. Keep straight along the right-hand hedgerow for a short distance, then cross another stile on the right. Walk along the right-hand fence line, through the gate in the far corner of the field, and continue, with a stream to your right. Go through another two gates, and return through the farmyard to Sollers Hope Church

# Ashton-under-Hill to Elmley Castle

〜 Approximately 6 miles 〜

*A gentle outward walk, with views across the Vale of Evesham, followed by a more strenuous return with spectacular views from Bredon Hill.*

### Parking

OS Map 150 Ref SO9937. The small car park opposite the Star Inn.

### Further Exploration

The inner ramparts of Elmley Castle Iron-Age Camp at the top of the hill cover 11 acres. The 18th-century tower, known as 'Parson's Folly' was built as a summer house and lookout to bring the height of the reputedly 961ft hill up to 1000ft.

**C**ross the road and go along the pavement past the school. Shortly, turn left up Wood Lane, keeping ahead at the end along a track to a stile. Continue across a young plantation, then along the bottom edge of the wood to a stile and keep following the wood round to the left. Beyond the wood, proceed along the edge of the field towards a house, passing through a gap to reach a wooden bridge in the corner of the field below the house. Follow the ridges uphill, passing the house on your right, to a gate and a lane. Turn left and go through the farmyard, turning right at the end past the barns to a field gate, then continue to another gate. Walk straight across the field to a gap in the hedge, then across the next field to the right of an oak tree to meet a bridleway. Bear slightly right towards the far corner of the field, go through the gap in the hedge, over a little bridge and straight across another field. Jump the stream, follow the line of trees round the left side of the field to a stile, cross the paddock and take the path through the churchyard to the village street. Turn right along the road opposite the Queen Elizabeth pub and then bear left over the green to the Old Mill.

# Old Mill Inn (Free House)

Located up a quiet 'no-through road' and backing onto a fine old mill, this pleasant pub has a large L-shaped bar with a few huge old beams,and a good collection of prints and photographs with a 'horse' theme adorning the walls, French doors lead out to a paved terrace and beer garden - ideal for summer drinking. Children and dogs are welcome.

On draught: Bass, Mitchells and Butlers, a guest beer, Murphy's, McEwan lager, Becks, Strongbow and Woodpecker cider. Food: the menu includes daily specials and a popular Sunday lunch carvery as well as popular standards like beefburger, bap and chips (£3), ploughman's (£3.75), pizza (£3.95), cod and chips (£4.95), filled baguettes (£3.75), and a choice of steaks (from (£7.50) in the evening; times are 12-2pm (Sun from 12.30pm) and 7-10pm (no food on Sun evening or Mon all day).

Telephone: 0386 710407.

St Mary's Church in Elmley Castle is worth a visit to see the 17th-century, life-size alabaster effigies on the tomb of the Savage family and some very old animal carvings in the porch.

**Little Comberton,**

1½ miles north of Elmley Castle, boasts one of the largest pigeon houses in the country, a round tower located in the farmyard of Nash's farm.

Go back to the Queen Elizabeth pub and walk up the lane beside it for about a mile to Hill House Farm, then proceed up the bridleway to a gate. Keep to the main stony track uphill to a stile. Cross and take the waymarked footpath left, following the grassy track uphill again to a gate and enter woodland. Turn right here along a track if you wish to visit the Iron -Age Camp on the ridge summit. If not, keep ahead, and on emerging from the wood, go left along the track past the masts on the edge of the wooded escarpment. After quarter of a mile ignore the marked track off to the left and at the end of the trees go through a gate and follow the waymarked path (Wychavon Way). Stay on this established path, which eventually heads steeply downhill through gates and over stiles to the village church. Turn left at the main road back to your car.

# Knucklas to Llanfair Waterdine

⊷ Approximately 5½ miles ⊶

*This walk takes you along the river valley on ancient tracks through pasture and woodland and over windswept hillsides. The return journey includes a long, steep climb.*

**Parking**

OS Map 137 Ref SO2574. Space may be found close to the village stores, otherwise head for the main road and end of the lane to Monaughty Poeth.

**W**alk towards Monaughty Poeth, over the River Teme and turn left towards Llanfair Waterdine. In just over half a mile, opposite a white house, turn right uphill to a farm. On reaching the farm, turn right through a metal gate and along a track down to a partly derelict cottage on your left. Pass this and turn immediately left through a gateway and follow the indistinct track alongside some nut trees through two gates and a gateway to a road. Turn left uphill, then, at a T-junction, turn right onto a rough track, soon turning left through a metal gate to follow another old track uphill. At the top go through a gate and follow the fence line down to another gate, then work around the top of the wood, keeping it on your left, proceed downhill and cross a stile. Bear half-right across a field, through a gateway, then immediately left through another gate and follow a track down to the road by Nantiago House. Turn right, shortly passing the post office, to the pub.

# Red Lion (Free House)

Believed to be almost 400 years old, this is a delightful traditional pub with a lounge bar complete with inglenook fireplace and brick-floored taproom with darts and table skittles. Children and dogs are permitted in the beer garden only.

On draught: Marston's Pedigree, Tetley Traditional, Ansell's Dark Mild and Pale Ale, Skol and Strongbow cider. Food: a wide range of bar meals may include excellent home-made soups, fried chicken, scampi, or plaice and chips (£2.25-£4.50). Evening meals can offer more adventurous choices, especially if advance notice is given; times are 12-1.30pm (except Tuesday when the pub is closed during the day), 7-9pm (except Sunday).

Telephone: 0547 528214.

**Further Exploration**

The small Marcher towns of Knighton, Leintwardine and Clun are all in easy reach of exploration, as is Offa's Dyke long-distance path if more serious walking seems attractive.

Turn left out of the pub, passing the village church, and after about quarter of a mile, turn left through a gate, down to the River Teme and cross over the footbridge. Turn left alongside the river, though a gate and walk half-right across the field to a gate and a road. Cross the road and pass through two gates, then cross Goytre farmyard (yellow arrows) to another gate, from which you now climb the well defined footpath up the very steep hillside. At the top of the hill, go through a gate, bear left at a crossing of paths to another gate and soon descend a good track into the valley. Near the bottom of the hill, bear right and continue round a hairpin bend to pass under a railway bridge. As you reach the farm buildings of Lower Hall Farm, bear left, passing in front of a diesel tank and go through the gate into fields. In the fourth field, bear left to a stile and go over the railway line. Go uphill onto a track, through a gate, past a house on your right, then turn right onto a good track. Pass through two more gates onto a road, turn right following the track downhill back into Knucklas and your car.

# Cleobury Mortimer to Hopton Wafers

∽ Approximately 6 miles ∽

*A gently undulating
ramble across open
farmland and through
lush meadowland
beside small brooks.*

**Parking**
OS Map 138 Ref SO6775. Free
car park in town centre

From the car park join the High Street via the archway beside the Stables Inn, turn right and shortly turn left onto a lane signposted to Milson. Remain on the quiet lane for a mile before turning right into a narrow lane, pass a farmhouse on the right then take a track on the left down to a metal gate. Follow the left-hand hedge to a stile, cross, and walk round the left-hand edge of the next field to a stile and footbridge. Head up the third field towards some farm buildings. Bear right onto a lane, then immediately left and cross a stile on the right, close to a bungalow. Follow yellow arrows on stiles across fields, eventually joining a lane where you bear left, cross a stream and pass Ditton Mill. Go uphill a short way to a gate into a camping ground on the right. Follow the waymarked path along its left-hand edge to a stile and follow the yellow arrows across fields and stiles to the main road. Turn right downhill to the pub.

## Crown (Free House)

This attractive creeper-clad inn, with its picturesque duckpond, is surrounded by terraces of tables for al fresco eating and drinking. Inside, the intimate bar - The Rent Room - is attractively decorated and has a large inglenook fireplace as well as a wood-burning stove. Comfortable seating includes armchairs and cushioned settles; oil paintings and prints adorn the walls. Children are allowed in the bar if eating - children's portions are available .

On draught: Bass, Boddingtons, Brains Dark, Flowers Original, Heineken, Stella Artois, Dry Blackthorn and Woodpecker ciders. Food: appetising bar food may offer dishes like carrot and orange soup (£2.15), sandwiches (from £1.75), game pie (£6.25), monkfish with lemon and lime sauce (£6.95) and celery and cashew risotto (£4.25). There is also a more formal restaurant dinner priced at £19.75 a head; times are 12-2pm and 7-9.30pm (until 10pm on Saturday, 9pm on Sunday).

Telephone: 0299 270372.

Turn right along the lane beside the pub, bear right at the school and follow the lane over a bridge and uphill past Hopton Court. At the next right-hand bend, cross the stile on the left (yellow marker) and keep to the hedge to another stile. Cross the lane onto a track and where it bears left towards a barn, go through the gate ahead. Head downhill through two more gates before bearing half-left across a large field to a gate (to the left of an underground water reservoir). Cross a lane and follow the arrowed path through three gates towards a farm. Cross a stile near the red-brick house and remain on the path to join the farm driveway. Turn right at the road, go through the next gate on the left, and cross two fields to climb a stile into school grounds. Exit at the lower end of the grounds, turn right onto the road, then take the next left back to the car park.

# Longville to Cardington
∾ Approximately 4½ miles ∾

*A gentle walk across meadowland beneath the impressive Caer Caradoc and Hope Bowdler hills.*

**Parking**

OS Map 137 Ref SO5293. A pull-in off the road one mile south-west of Longville in the dale (near a petrol station).

**F**rom the end of the pull-in (towards Longville) go along the road to the crossroads, turning left to East Wall Farm. At the farm, bear left over a stream and continue to a cluster of houses. Turn right through a gate onto an established track and go on through gates until the track bears left. Here, keep straight on beside the hedge to the left of a field. Where the hedge bears sharp left, continue straight across the field, through two gates onto a narrow road. Turn right past Stone Cottage and walk along the road for quarter of a mile to a marked footpath on the left, leading to an old cottage. Just past the cottage, turn left, over a footbridge and stile, onto a waymarked path. Shortly, turn right through a holly hedge, then follow the yellow route across fields and stiles, parallel to the stream, into Cardington. On reaching the road bear right downhill to the pub.

## Royal Oak (Free House)

Built in 1462, this cottage-style pub nestles into the hillside just below the church. The low beams, massive walls and big inglenook fireplace make it a perfect setting on bleak winter days as well as fine summer ones. Children are welcome, but in the evening only if they are eating. Dogs are permitted, but only at the discretion of the landlord.

On draught: Wadworth 6X, Bass, M&B Springfield, Guinness, Carling Black Label, Strongbow cider. Food: the extensive menu is frequently changed and may include, beside the usual ploughman's (£3.20), fidget pie (£3.35), lasagne (£3.95), chicken cobbler (£5.60) or cauliflower cheese (£2.65); times are 12-2pm and 7-8.30pm (not Sun evening). Pub closed Mon (except BHs).

Telephone: 06943 266.

From the pub, turn left to the junction immediately ahead and turn right uphill following the road past a crossroads and Court Farm. Shortly, turn right through the first gate, then head straight across a field and across a stream to a new fence. Keeping it on your left, go through a gate near a derelict house, follow the fence line for about 200 yards to a stile on your left. Cross it and follow a line of new trees, then go through two gates and, with a fence on the left, cross the field, aiming towards a pylon on the skyline, to a gate by a holly tree. Go through and turn left following the field boundary round to the right to pass through a little gate at the base of a big tree in the corner of the field. Bear left, following the edge of this next field to a fence stile, then go slightly left across the following field for about 200 yards to a bridge over a stream. Bear right to a broken tree and then proceed down to farm buildings, keeping to the fence. Go through a gate, and the farm to another gate before turning left onto the road past East Wall Farm to retrace your steps to the car.

# Horsey to Winterton-on-Sea

### ∾ Approximately 8 miles ∾

*Though long, this walk is very easy and flat, the return taking you along the wild dunes of the Norfolk Coast.*

**Parking**
OS Map 134 Ref TG4522. Car park near windmill (£1 fee in summer)

**Further Exploration**
Horsey Windpump
This restored windmill is a notable landmark and overlooks Horsey Mere and marshes, noted for their wild birds and insects.Both Mere and Mill are National Trust properties.

Thrigby Hall Wildlife Gardens, Filby
A few minutes' away by car, the 250-year-old park of Thrigby Hall is now the home to animals and birds from Asia. The lake has ornamental wildfowl, there are tropical and bird houses, a 'willow pattern' garden, and a fascinating crocodile swamp..
Telephone: 0493 369477.

Turn right out of the car park and follow the road until you reach a stile on the right (footpath sign). Cross this and follow the path all the way round to the left until it rejoins the road. Turn rightand when you reach the second curve of the 'S' bend take the public footpath signposted on the left just after Ivy House. Follow this path until you reach a stile. Cross this, turn left onto the lane and follow it round to the right, always keeping to the right until you reach the high walled garden of Burnley Hall. Here turn left and follow the road, keeping to the left, past the White House and onto a track. Follow the track until you can see some allotment gardens on your right. Just before these you will see a path leading towards a church. At the end of this path turn left onto Black Street and continue past the village green until you reach The Lane on the right. You will find the pub a short distance up on the left.

Turn right out of the pub, cross Black Street into the Market Place and continue up North Market Road. When you reach the sand dunes, you will find the coastal path slightly to the left near the fence. Follow the path up the coast for some way, passing two fenced-off concrete access points to the beach on your right. At the second one, turn left onto a track. When it eventually meets a lane, keep to the right and follow the lane past a pub on the right up to another road. Follow this road in the same direction, keeping to the left until you arrive back at the car park.

# Fishermans Return (Manns)

Formerly a row of fishermen's cottages, this traditional brick-and-flint Norfolk pub is about 300 years old. The wood-panelled public bar is decorated with old prints and photographs of local scenes, and is warmed in winter by a cast iron wood-burner. The smaller lounge has low ceilings and an open fireplace, and the family room,, with pool table and other games, leads to a large enclosed garden.

On draught: Adnams Southwold, Webster's Yorkshire, Norwich Mild, Courage Directors, Guinness, Beamish, and various lagers and ciders. Food: daily specials such as game and vegetable stockpot (£2.50), Hungarian goulash (£4.75) and seafood tagliatelle (£4.75), supplement pub favourites like toasted sandwiches (from £1.20), jacket potatoes (from £1.75), roast chicken (£4), Dover sole (£9.50) and steaks (from £9). Home-made puddings (£1.75) may include bread and butter pudding and fruit crumble; times are 12-2pm and 7-9.30pm

Telephone: 0493 393305.

# West Acre to Castle Acre

~ Approximately 5½ miles ~

*A gentle walk through undulating farmland and woodland in the River Nar valley, with views of the magnificent ruins at Castle Acre.*

### Parking

OS Map 132 Ref TF7815. Park on common land by the ford sign at a sharp right-hand bend on the South Acre to Narborough lane.

### Further Exploration

### Castle Acre

This delightful little village seems very lively for such a small place, no doubt largely because of the attraction of its magnificent ruined priory and castle. The priory dates back to Norman times and fell into ruin in the 16th century after the Dissolution of the Monasteries. A particularly impressive remnant is the glorious arcaded west front of the priory church, a reminder of past splendour.

From the car, walk down the lane, then just before the ford climb the stile on your right and follow the fenced footpath. Cross two bridges and enter a field. The footpath bears to the right to a gate and enters a wood. Now on a track, pass through the edge of the wood, then across open marshy ground. At the end of the track, go through a gate and turn right onto another track, which leads you towards Castle Acre. On reaching the edge of the village, turn right towards the priory ruins, then shortly left into the main street. The pub lies to your left.

Leave the pub, turn left, then right through a flint arch and head downhill towards the river bridge. Just before the bridge turn right into Blind Lane. Take the left-hand fork, then at a T-junction in front of the priory ruins, turn left and cross the ford. At the road junction ahead, turn left for a short distance to where the road bears round to the left, and here keep straight ahead to follow a broad track towards a pylon. On reaching a crossroads of tracks, turn right and follow this path for nearly two miles, then turn right on reaching a blue waymark (not too obvious) on a post in the corner of a field. Head downhill, passing under the power lines, eventually reaching a road. Turn right along the road and after rounding a sharp right-hand bend you will see the common land where you parked your car at the top of the lane, on the left.

## Ostrich (Greene King)

This large, rambling old pub has a spacious, welcoming front bar beyond which is the eating area. This family room, with its high ceiling, brickwork, beams and open fire, suggests that the building may once have been an old hall. There is a door to the garden which has plenty of picnic tables, and several aviaries.

On draught: Greene King IPA, Rayments, Mild and Abbot Ale, Kronenbourg 1666, Harp, Taunton cider. Food: the menu includes standard pub favourites such as ploughman's (from £2.20), sandwiches (from £1), omelettes (from £2.75), grills (from £4.75), pizzas (from £1.70) and salads (from £4.30); times are 12-2pm and 7-10.30pm. Telephone: 0760 755398.

# Pulham Market to Tivetshall St Mary

$\sim$ Approximately 4½ miles $\sim$

*This is a pleasant, gentle, farmland and village walk.*

**Parking:**
OS Map 156 Ref TM1986.
Pulham Market Church.

**Further Exploration**
**Banham Zoo and Appleyard Craft Court**
Situated in 25 acres of parkland and garden, this zoo specialises in rare and endangered species of animals and birds. There is also an indoor activity centre and a craft courtyard.
Telephone: 095387 771.

**Bressingham Steam Museum and Gardens**
Here there are three steam-hauled trains, two running through five miles of the wooded Waveney Valley and one running through two miles of Europe's largest hardy plant nursery. There are also six acres of delightful gardens.
Telephone: 037988 386 & 382.

From the church, walk along Guildhall Lane, then after half a mile, when you reach a right-hand bend follow the waymarked path diagonally left downhill. Go through the gap in the hedge and turn left towards the stream. Walk parallel with the stream through fields, until you reach a concrete slab and tractor crossing. Beyond this and a further crossing, turn immediately right around the edge of the field and cross the ditch at the gap in the hedge. Keep left in the next field and head towards the solitary cottage (not the farmhouse to your right) on the busy main road. Cross the A140 and take the footpath to the left of Turnpike Cottage. Head towards the village, following the edge of the field round to the right to a farm track. Just before the track joins School Road, turn left along the waymarked footpath which eventually leads to the rear of a row of houses. Go across a ditch (can be very wet and muddy) and pass through the left-hand corner of a garden on a defined path, then cross another bridge into a paddock before reaching a road. Turn left along Rectory Road and lef tagain into Tinkers Lane. At Ram Lane turn left for the pub.

Leave the pub and turn right along the A140 for 60 yards, then turn left onto a lane signposted Semere Green. Go round the bend and shortly turn left along a farm track. Follow this along the edge of the field until you can cross the ditch. With the hedge on the left, soon join another footpath and bear right. Pulham Market will shortly come into view. When you reach a farm track leading to the hall, turn left towards it and then go over a stile on the right. Keep the perimeter fence of the hall to your right and follow it all the way down to the entranceto the hall at the main road. Turn left along the road to return to the church.

# Old Ram (Free House)

This rambling old coaching inn dates back to the 17th century and the bar is divided into individual areas, each with heavy beams, standing timbers and brick floors. A huge log fire warms the main bar which is decorated with antique tools. The cosy side rooms are comfortably furnished, some with sofas and an intimate dining room has pews, a wood-burning stove and a gallery. Children are welcome. Five bedrooms offer overnight accommodation.

On draught: Adnams Bitter, Greene King Abbot, Woodfordes Nelson's Revenge, Ruddles County, and a guest beer. There are also decent house wines and several malt whiskies. Food: popular bar food includes a breakfast menu, served from 9am, and a printed menu with dishes like steak and kidney pie, chilli, aubergine and mushroom bake and moussaka (from £5.25), salmon steaks (£7.95), ham salad (£5.25), ploughman's (£3.95), burgers (£3.50) and a selection of puddings (£2.50).Times are 9am-10pm (Sun, 9.30pm).

Telephone: (0379) 608228.

# Holme next the Sea to Thornham

### ∽ Approximately 6 miles ∾

*An easy and interesting coastal walk alongside the North Holme Nature Reserve. Watch out for rare species of migratory birds.*

**Parking**

OS Map 132 Ref TF6944. Car park fee 50p per day

**Further Exploration**

Holme Nature Reserve

This is administered by the Norfolk Naturalists Trust and non-members have to pay an entry fee. Varied habitats include dunes, saltmarsh, brackish and fresh water pools, which make this site a paradise for a range of wildlife. Permits may be obtained to visit the Holme Bird Observatory Reserve which was established in 1962 on 7 acres of pine and scrub-covered dunes, and where the study of migratory birds is carried out daily. There are 5 hides for use by visitors, and a 10-post nature trail designed for families, as well as a nature garden and a pond. Telephone: 0485 25240.

Leave the car park from the entrance and bear right, heading towards the sea. When you reach the path running along the coast, at a slightly higher level than the beach, turn right. This path is marked with yellow arrows, and there are information signs at various points along the route telling you about the reserve and the flora and fauna to be seen. Follow the path along the coast and then inland as you approach Thornham. When the path meets a road used by yachtsmen and others visiting the small marina, turn right and the pub is straight ahead.

When you leave the pub, you can go back along the same path, or return along the beach.

## Lifeboat Inn (Free House)

Built in the late 1500s, this pub has a well-documented history of offering a warm haven to smugglers and travellers alike. The two small bars have low ceilings, beams and dark wooden furniture, and there is a large eating area at the back, a separate restaurant, and a courtyard with many picnic tables and a play area for children. Situated next to a campsite, this pub gets extremely busy during the summer, especially at weekends. There are 13 ensuite bedrooms.

On draught: Greene King IPA and Abbot Ale, guest ale, Kronenbourg 1664, Harp, Carlsberg. Food: a very wide range of snacks and main meals, served in generous portions, may include home-made soups, from £1.90, pies from £5.25, many fresh fish dishes from £5.95; times are 12-2pm and 7-10pm. The restaurant (booking essential) opens at 7pm, and a meal à la carte costs from £25 a head or there is a fixed-price menu at £17.50.

Telephone: 0485 26236.

# Dunwich Cliffs to Eastbridge

~ Approximately 5 miles ~

Start your walk from the back of the car park, taking the track nearest the public convenience building and head downhill towards the water. Follow the path away from the sea, through the woods, following the curve of the water but keeping it to your left. At a T-junction, turn left, cross a stile and head towards another junction. Turn left again, and when you reach a road, cross straight over and continue along the track up and down Hangman's Hill. When the path joins the road, keep straight to arrive at the pub.

*A delightful walk which takes you through farmland, woodland, heathland and along the seashore. If you take your binoculars you may see some rare birds, as the route borders the Minsmere Nature Reserve.*

## Eel's Foot (Adnams)

This is a very small, unpretentious pub with friendly staff and a happy, relaxed atmosphere. There are lots of tables in the garden, and swings for the active. Dogs are welcome in the bar with the landlord's permission.

On draught: Adnams, Beamish, Carling Black Label, Red Stripe and scrumpy. Food: the menu includes dishes like chicken and mushroom pie, steak and kidney pie (both £3.80), sausage and chips (£2.30), cod and chips (£3.40) and homemade vegetarian dishes (from £3.80); times are 11.45-2pm and 6-11pm.

Telephone: 0728 830154.

Turn left out of the pub and, at Rose Cottage, follow the sign pointing left 'To the Sluice'. This path takes you through farmland, over stiles and gates (all marked) down to the sea. At the shore, turn left and, depending on the weather, you can either walk along the shore or behind the dunes. Sometimes, in the breeding season, parts of the dunes are roped off so you will have to take the beach. Head for the white National Trust building on the cliff, and you will soon reach the car park.

**Parking**

OS Map 156 Ref TM4767
National Trust car park (£1, free to members).

**Further Exploration**

Minsmere Nature Reserve (RSPB)

This bird sanctuary is one of the most important in Europe. For non-members, there is a public hide whose entrance is near The Sluice - don't forget your binoculars!

Dunwich Cliffs

This is a popular spot for hang-gliders, but for the less adventurous there are the National Trust Shop and Tea Rooms.

# Iken to Snape

~ Approximately 5 miles ~

*A gentle walk by the River Alde, with pretty views of marshes and saltings. Many sea and river birds can be seen here.*

**Parking**

OS Map 156 Ref TM4056. Iken Cliffs car park.

**Further Exploration**

Snape Maltings

These Victorian buildings, originally used to malt barley, now house the renwned music school and concert hall set up by Sir Benjamin Britten and Sir Peter Pears, and there are also various craft, kitchen and garden shops, an art gallery, restaurant and tea shop. In the summer there is a programme of activity holidays, and river trips from Snape Quay are a relaxing way to see the river.

Telephone: 072888 303.

Aldeburgh

This delightful seaside town is only a few minutes away by car. There are some beautiful buildings, a charming seafront, and an interesting Museum.

Begin your walk by finding the footpath at the bottom left-hand corner of the car park. This is mainly a planked path of railway sleepers, and it runs beside the marshes with farmland to the left and the river to the right. When you reach a fork in the path, keep to the left until you reach a road. There, turn right and walk past the front of Snape Maltings and over the bridge. Turn right immediately after the bridge and follow the river wall to some woods and a yellow footpath sign. At this point, you may like to turn right and wander down to the river's edge, but make sure you return to this spot. Turn left at the yellow sign (or straight on if you have been down to the river), and keep to the well-trodden path until you eventually meet another established and signposted path to your left. Take this path - the Canser - and Snape Maltings will soon come into view on your left. At the end of this stretch of path, turn right and you will shortly reach a road. Turn left and the pub is on the next corner.

Turn left out of the pub and follow the roadside path back towards Snape Maltings. Having crossed over the bridge, turn immediately left and follow the path at the back of the Maltings, past the bronze sculpture, and head towards the avenue of trees. There are two paths to the left of this avenue: one running parallel to it to the left of the hedge, and one running at right angles. The latter follows the water's edge and does bring you back to the car park, but is only possible at low tide. Take the former, follow it as far as a T-junction and turn left towards the car park.

# Crown Inn (Adnams)

This is a super pub with lots of room inside and out. Wooden beams, old brick floors, open fires and old Suffolk settles add to the comfortable, relaxed atmosphere inside. The garden has a number of farmyard animals living at one end. The landlord and his staff are all very helpful and friendly.

On draught: stocks vary with the seasons; normally you will find Adnams Best, Southwold and Broadside, as well as Carlsberg lager and Beamish stout, with the addition of Mild and Tally Ho in winter, and a good cider in the summer. Food: generous portions of freshly made dishes are good value, for example, Scottish salmon with a red caviar and cream sauce (£7.50), chicken breast and leek pie (£5.50), and tagliatelle with creamy garlic mushrooms (£4.85), with a range of desserts (£2.50) from chocolate roulade to pecan and banana flan; times are as lunchtime opening, and evenings from 6pm.

Telephone: 0728 688324.

# Kettlebaston to Chelsworth

~ Approximately 4 miles ~

*There are some lovely views on this walk, but it is badly signposted, so you do need to concentrate.*

**Parking**

OS Map 155 Ref TL9650. Park at the widest point of the main road in Kettlebaston.

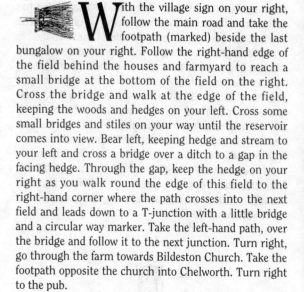

With the village sign on your right, follow the main road and take the footpath (marked) beside the last bungalow on your right. Follow the right-hand edge of the field behind the houses and farmyard to reach a small bridge at the bottom of the field on the right. Cross the bridge and walk at the edge of the field, keeping the woods and hedges on your left. Cross some small bridges and stiles on your way until the reservoir comes into view. Bear left, keeping hedge and stream to your left and cross a bridge over a ditch to a gap in the facing hedge. Through the gap, keep the hedge on your right as you walk round the edge of this field to the right-hand corner where the path crosses into the next field and leads down to a T-junction with a little bridge and a circular way marker. Take the left-hand path, over the bridge and follow it to the next junction. Turn right, go through the farm towards Bildeston Church. Take the footpath opposite the church into Chelworth. Turn right to the pub.

## Peacock Inn (Free House)

Within the walls of this unassuming 14th-century inn is a large comfortable bar with oak beams and an attractive stone inglenook fireplace. There is also a cosy lounge with some exposed Tudor brickwork, and a garden. Children are welcome in the dining area.

On draught: a wide selection of well kept real ales, featuring regularly changing guest beers. Food: freshly prepared by the resident chef, bar meals range from soups and ploughman's to the home-made pies which are the chef's speciality: for example, chicken and herbs in white wine sauce or steak and stout, served with local vegetables (around £5.75). Delicious puddings may include baked apples with mixed fruit and orange honey sauce (around £2.50); times are 12-2.30pm and 7-10pm (longer in summer). There is a separate restaurant.

Telephone: 0449 740758.

On leaving the pub, turn right to reach a track beside the Old School House. Follow this to the second footpath sign pointing left and aim for the gap in the trees, walking downhill to a ditch with a circular walk sign. Turn right and follow this path past a copse on the left, over a ditch, through a gate, and straight ahead, keeping the large mounds on your right. This is the reservoir of the outward route. Go through the farmyard (Waggers Farm) keeping to a wide track to a bridge. Immediately before the bridge, take the right-hand footpath and, keeping the water to your left, follow it to join a wider track leading to a road. Turn right here and you will soon be back in Kettlebaston.

# Manningtree to Dedham

⁓ Approximately 6 miles ⁓

*A popular walk through the countryside that inspired Constable to paint some of his finest and best-known works. The walk is very clearly signposted.*

### Parking

OS Map 168 Ref TM0932. Manningtree railway station.

### Further Exploration

Dedham

It is well worth dawdling round this pretty village before resuming your walk. Look out for the Elizabethan Free School, and the 16th-century church whose tower can be found in many of Constable's paintings. Sir Alfred Munnings, President of the Royal Academy from 1944-1949, also lived here and his house is now a gallery dedicated to his work.

From the front of the church, take the footpath in the left-hand corner of the field opposite. Follow this to a road, turn right, and a few yards further are two footpath signs pointing left: one crossing the field and the other following its perimeter (yellow circular walk sign). Follow the latter to reach a farm gate and join a wider track which takes you past a farmhouse. At the top of the slope take a path to the right and follow this downhill through some woods, over stiles and a railway track. Walk uphill through a series of paddocks linked by stiles and painted with white marks, eventually reaching a road. Cross this and a stile, then walk across the field diagonally to your left to another stile and a road. Turn right and keep on the road to a left-hand bend where there are two footpath signs. Follow the one on the left and walk across the fields towards a group of cottages, climbing the stile to their left, and continuing behind the gardens to a road. Cross to a small road ahead, pass an old house and cross playing fields with the church to your left to the main road almost opposite the pub.

# Marlborough Head (Ind Coope)

Set in beautiful 'Constable country', and opposite the painter's old school, this is a delightfully unspoilt 15th-century pub with several bars. There is some fine carved woodwork in the central lounge, and the Constable bar is beamed and furnished with wooden tables in alcoves. There is a garden with a patio and a children's play area.

On draught: Adnams, Benskins Best, Guinness and Lowenbrau. There are several wines on offer, ranging in price from £6.95 to £15.50 a bottle. Food: the vast and varied menu may include cream cheese and caviar sandwich (£2.50), ploughman's (£3.50), and rabbit casserole (£5.25). Several vegetarian dishes are always on offer, such as pine kernel and pumpkin seed risotto (.£4.50). Delicious desserts may include chocolate and brandy pot (£2.75) and fresh nectarine melba with cream (£2.50). All the food is home-cooked and the service is quick, friendly and efficient, even when busy; times are 12-2pm and 7-9.30pm.

Telephone: 0206 323124.

O n leaving the pub, retrace your steps out of the village. At the right-hand bend, bear left up the public footpath and follow this, over stiles, down to the river, where you turn right. Keep the water on your left at all times and follow the river until you cross a large concrete sluice. Take the left-hand path until you reach a circular walk signpost. Turn right, go under the railway bridge, then turn left up the track to head back towards the car park of Manningtree station.

**Flatford Mill (not open)**
Once the Constable family mill, this now houses a field-study centre. It is not open to the public, but large groups can arrange in advance to be shown around. Next to the mill, in Bridge Cottage, is a visitor centre, information on Constable, a tea room and a shop. Both the mill and cottage are owned by the National Trust. Telephone: 0206 298260.

**Willy Lott's Cottage (not open)**
A private house, this meticulously preserved cottage was one of Constable's most celebrated subjects and the home of one of his friends.

If you wish to see the countryside from a different angle, skiffs, rowing boats and canoes can be hired daily in season (Easter to Oct) from the Bridge Cottage (see above) or the boatyard in Mill Lane, Dedham.

# Clavering to Arkesden

~ Approximately 5 miles ~

*An easy, mainly flat walk through rural Essex, passing through two of the county's prettiest villages.*

**Parking**

OS Map 167 Ref TL4731. By the village green in Clavering.

**Further Exploration**

**Audley End House**

This is an English Heritage property just west of Saffron Walden and well worth a visit. It is an impressive stone building with beautifully landscaped gardens, where open air productions are often held in the summer. Telephone: 0799 22399.

From the car, walk along the footway beside the road, keeping the village green on your right until you reach the Cricketers pub. Bear left and follow the road to Arkesden, keeping the pub on your right. Turn left when you reach a path between the houses. The sign is obscured by a hedge, but it is opposite a terrace of cottages, two of which are thatched - if you reach a path to the right, you have gone too far. On emerging into a field, turn right and walk round the edge to a gap in the hedges. Turn right and continue up the side of the field to the top. Turn left here ('no horses' sign) and follow this path to a junction with a wide track, where you turn right. The path passes to the left of Wood Hall, then continues down the side of a field to Arkesden. On reaching the road, turn right to the pub.

# Axe and Compasses (Greene King)

This popular pub has a very comfortable main bar with armchairs in which to relax. Steps lead down to the large, beamed dining area, and a separate bar furnished with many interesting artefacts, wooden furniture, and a dartboard. The pub is part-thatched and has an outside seating area with attractive, rustic garden furniture, overlooking the village post office and shop.

On draught: Greene King IPA, Rayments, Abbot Ale and Kronenbourg 1664. There is a good selection of wine by the glass or bottle. Food: typical of the home-made dishes on the menu are soup of the day (£1.90), steak and kidney pie (£5.75), skate in batter (£5.75), spaghetti bolognese (£4.50)and a variety of pies and cheesecakes for dessert (£2.50). Vegetarians may find nut roast, vegetarian lasagne, or stuffed aubergines; times are 12-2pm and 7-9.30pm. There are barbecues in the garden on Sundays during the summer. Booking advisable.

Telephone: 0799 550272.

Turn left out of the pub and follow the narrow main road through Arkesden. At the end of the line of houses, take the public footpath on the left, signposted to Chardwell Farm. Go along the left-hand edge of the field, keeping the woods and hedge to your left to a double track and a 'no horses' sign. Turn right along the track, shortly to leave it at a right-hand bend onto a footpath. Proceed ahead to the right of the hedge, pass between some gardens, beside a cottage and emerge onto common land. Take the footpath on your right, cross the road, pass between two cottages (can be muddy), and head straight across open farmland via two stiles to another road. Turn left and follow the road through a village to the B1038 and the Fox and Hounds pub. Cross to the pub, walk through the car park to a stile and proceed uphill. Turn left downhill, pass a cottage, go over a small bridge, then head down back to the village green.

# Swavesey to Fen Drayton

∾ Approximately 5 miles ∾

*A pleasant short walk, mainly on broad firm tracks in typical fenland landscape. Very easy walking.*

**Parking**
OS Map 154 Ref TL3669.
Swavesey church car park

**Further exploration**
The Cambridgeshire St Ives is an attractive small market town on the River Ouse. On Bank Holiday Mondays the entire town shuts down in favour of a huge street market.

The university city of Cambridge, with its ancient colleges, fine parks and superb museums, is only 8 miles away, and the village of Grantchester, made famous by Rupert Brooke's poem of that name, is only 2 miles south-west of the city.

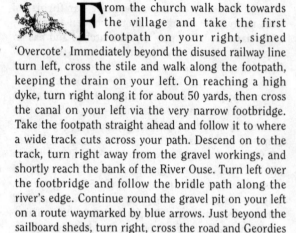

From the church walk back towards the village and take the first footpath on your right, signed 'Overcote'. Immediately beyond the disused railway line turn left, cross the stile and walk along the footpath, keeping the drain on your left. On reaching a high dyke, turn right along it for about 50 yards, then cross the canal on your left via the very narrow footbridge. Take the footpath straight ahead and follow it to where a wide track cuts across your path. Descend on to the track, turn right away from the gravel workings, and shortly reach the bank of the River Ouse. Turn left over the footbridge and follow the bridle path along the river's edge. Continue round the gravel pit on your left on a route waymarked by blue arrows. Just beyond the sailboard sheds, turn right, cross the road and Geordies Bridge and keep on this broad track into Fen Drayton, where the pub is at the far end of the village on the left.

## Three Tuns ( Greene King)

This delightful old timbered pub is a very comfortable, welcoming village local where the heavily beamed bars are warmed by inglenook fireplaces. At the rear there is a small garden with interesting-looking play equipment for children.

On draught: Greene King IPA and Abbot Ale. Food: generous portions of good food are the hallmark of this fairly short menu with dishes from about £4 to £5 - for example cold meat with pickles, salad and baked potato or chips, lasagne with salad or potatoes, and plaice. Puddings are around £2 and there is a traditional Sunday lunch. Times are 11.30am-1.30pm (Sun from 12 noon).
Telephone: 0954 30242

O n leaving the pub, turn right and retrace your steps towards Low Fen. At the edge of the village, turn right onto the footpath signposted 'Swavesey'. Shortly, cross a drain and a private road, then pass the windmill and craft workshop on your right. The road curves sharply to the right, passing the cemetery on the edge of Swavesey. On reaching Taylors Lane, turn left and follow the lane to the main road, where you turn left again to return to the church and your car.

# Ashdon to Bartlow

∽ Approximately 6 miles ∽

*A gently undulating
walk on well worn
tracks with good views
of the Essex and
Cambridgeshire
countryside.*

**Parking**

OS Map 154 Ref TL5841. In the
lane leading up to All Saints'
Church

**Further Exploration**

Linton Zoological Gardens
The zoo has been open since
1972 and has a large collection
of leopards, pumas, panthers,
vultures, macaws, snakes, bird-
eating spiders and many other
creatures.
Telephone 0223 891308

Walk round to the left of the church and turn left onto the grassy path in the field, keeping the houses away to your right. Cross to a stile and a track. Turn left and continue, with the fence to your left, up the side of a field to a road. Cross, and climb the steps to walk on the cycle track. Turn right and keep parallel with the road towards Ashdon. When the path meets the road, cross and follow the public footpath sign opposite. Walk over the plank bridge, then go straight ahead up towards a single house, then round to its right to a road where you turn left and fairly soon right, up Kates Lane. After about half a mile, beyond a large house on your right, turn left on the footpath, over a stream, then up across the field. Turn right at the top, then left at the corner, and join the narrow road between houses and a windmill down to the main road. Turn right here, then left through white gates (sign obscured by a tree) and up a drive. Where the drive forks, follow the footpath, bearing slightly left between an avenue of trees. At a junction of arrowed paths, take the one straight ahead. At the far corner of the large field, turn left downhill with a hedge to your right, then turn right along the side of a wood. This track takes you under an old railway bridge, over a brook, and up to a road. Turn left here, then left at the junction, and you will soon see the pub.

# Three Hills (Greene King)

This is a large, handsome 15th-century pub whose comfortable bar features oak beams, polished brasses, and a log fire burning within an inglenook fireplace. There is also a well-tended walled garden and vine-covered terrace A popular establishment, it soon becomes busy, but service is efficient and friendly. Children are welcome in the garden and restaurant.

On draught: Abbot Ale, IPA, Rayments and Kronenbourg 1664. Food: bar meals range from soup and sandwiches (from £1.55) to trout in almonds (£7.95), gammon (£6.25) and lamb cutlets (£5.95), with desserts from £2.20; times are 12-1.45pm and 7-9.30pm. Vegetarian dishes are also available and on Sunday a set lunch at £8.35.

Telephone: 0223 891259.

**Audley End**
1½ miles west of Saffron Walden, the magnificent Jacobean manor house built by Thomas Howard, Earl of Suffolk, is well worth a visit. Its landscaped grounds were designed by Capability Brown and, as a modern touch, contain a miniature railway. Open Apr to 1st Sun in Oct.
Telephone 0799 522399

Turn left on to the road after leaving the pub and take the first road right towards Hadstock. Pass the disused railway line and take the track off to the left which gradually climbs uphill and bears right to a hedge at the end of a field. Turn left here and walk downhill to a junction of tracks where you turn right, keeping the wood on your left and go uphill again for about 3/4 mile. As the track veers to the right, you will see Bowsers Farm ahead, but before you reach the buildings, turn sharp left and follow the track by the brook and over the gate at the bottom into a field. Go through the gate to your left at the bottom corner of the field, over the brook, (not the gate straight ahead), and head for another gate across the field. Through this, turn right on to the road, walk up the hill and turn right through a white gate opposite a large house on your left. This brings you to the footpath/cycletrack above the road. Turn right, pass a brick-and-flint building on your right, and the church is on your left.

# Lode to Horningsea

∽ Approximately 6½ miles ∽

*A very pretty walk on well-worn paths, very popular with walkers and joggers.*

**Parking**
OS Map 154 Ref TL5362. Anglesey Abbey National Trust car park. Be sure to note what time the car park closes!

**Further Exploration**
**Anglesey Abbey and Gardens**
Built around 1600 on the site of an Augustinian Abbey, the house is home to the Fairhaven collection of paintings and furniture. The beautiful 100 acre garden was laid out this century, and incorporates the Lode watermill. Telephone 0223 811200.

**Cambridge**
Just a few minutes away by car, the heart of this ancient university city is the row of colleges which lines the River Cam and overlooks the Backs.

Find the footpath at the rear left-hand corner of the car park and follow the yellow arrows to a mill and over a small footbridge. Take the footpath straight ahead and bear right alongside a spinney, until you come to a disused railway track. Turn left into this and shortly take a right-hand track (yellow arrow). At the end of this, turn left and follow the yellow arrows round the perimeter of the fields, over a little bridge and stile, straight ahead until you reach a gate and a signpost saying 'Horningsea circular walk' and pointing to a clump of trees on the right. Forgetting the yellow arrows now, go through the clump of trees past a fishing lake, and over a stile at the far end, follow the track beside the field leading towards the pylon. Turn left under the pylon and the track widens and eventually leads into a lay-by on the main road of Horningsea. Turn left and the pub is at the other end of the village on the right, opposite a garden centre (about three-quarters of a mile).

Turn left out of the pub, to a signpost in the hedge on the right-hand side of the road next to the speed-limit sign. Follow the path across the fields towards Allicky Farm straight ahead. Follow the track that runs to the left of the farm and then over the disused railway to a road. Turn left and a short way along is a bridge (you don't need to cross this, but do notice the pretty view of the other side). Go left over the stile and follow the path on the left of the water which leads all the way to the mill. At the mill, turn right and follow the yellow arrows right again back to the car park.

# Plough & Fleece (Greene King)

A lot larger than it looks from the outside, this friendly and very popular pub has built on a no-smoking dining area. The cosy lounge is comfortably furnished, while the public bar has enormous character with high-backed settles and wooden tables, oak beams and a red-tiled floor. There is also a pretty garden with a children's play area. Children not permitted indoors.

On draught: IPA, Abbot, Kronenbourg, Harp, Guinness, Dry Blackthorn cider. Food: delicious home-made dishes served in generous portions, may include Stilton and broccoli flan (£2.90), Suffolk hotpot (£4.50), Welsh fish pie (£5.40) and Beef Wellington (£10). Self-indulgent desserts cost about £2.10; times are 12-2pm (Sun 1.30pm) and 7-9.30pm (no food Sun and Mon).

Telephone: 0223 860795.

**Newmarket**

The centre of the 'sport of kings' since 1605, this is the headquarters of British horse racing. For an opportunity to see the horses at work on the historic gallops, at home in the yards, on the racecourse and at the National Stud, book a tour at the National Horseracing Museum.

Telephone 0638 667333.

**Wicken Fen**

Here visitors can enjoy 600 acres of wetland nature reserve, rich in plant and insect life. Built with traditional materials, Fen Cottage, furnished in 1930s style, is also open,

Telephone 0353 720274.

# Winster to Birchover

 Approximately 4½ miles 

*A hilly walk with some short, sharp climbs, some superb rock scenery and occasional sighting of deer, particularly in winter.*

**Parking**

OS Map 119 Ref SK2460. In the village of Winster along Main Street.

**Further Exploration**

Winster

This is probably the best surviving 18th-century mining settlement in the Peak, most of Main Street being of this age. The 17th-century Market Hall is now a National Trust information office.

Almost opposite the telephone kiosk in Main Street is Woodhouse Lane leading to a footpath signposted to Birchover. Go downhill, through an iron gate and soon a slabbed path bears left off the main track and along the hillside. Follow the intermittent slabs, pass through a squeeze stile, then a gap in the hedge and continue into and out of a shallow valley towards a lone tree and a stile. Climb steadily through a succession of three squeeze stiles, the final one being in the top left-hand corner of the field, near an electricity pole. This brings you to a minor road. Turn right and climb steeply up a narrow lane. Just over the brow of the hill, note a pair of stocks on the left-hand side. You will now see Birchover ahead. Reach the main street, turn left, walk through the village to the Druid, the second pub, on the right.

Retrace your steps along the road and follow the gentle climb back through the village. Pass the site of an ancient pinfold on the right, and opposite a light industrial unit, turn right onto a black-surfaced track. After Barn Farm on the left, a squeeze stile brings you to a three-fingered signpost. Go through a gap in hedge on the left, then keep ahead to arrive at the head of a wooded valley. Follow the fence marking newly planted trees, and a more mature wood and, when clear of trees, go straight across the field to a hedge bordering a lane. Follow this stony lane downhill, and at a junction with the drive to Sabine Hey, turn right by Clough Wood, then right again through a gap by a gate. Pass through some overgrown mineral workings, then at the base of the slope take the first track right which follows a discoloured stream, and goes through an area of overgrown undergrowth and trees. Cross the stream by a footbridge and head diagonally across the field to a pair of stone uprights, then to a stile marked with a white-painted pole. Cross a second complicated stile and head up to the road. Turn right to return to Winster.

# Druid Inn (Free House)

This creeper-covered, 200-year-old pub beneath the Rowter Rocks, has one bar with several rooms, including a fairly modern extension. It is warmed by coal fires, the furniture is plain but comfortable, and the decor is traditionally simple. In front of the building is a terrace with tables. Children are allowed up to 8pm if eating. No dogs.

On draught: Mansfield, John Smith's, Magnet, Murphy's, Fosters, Strongbow cider. Food: the international menu may include Cantonese spare ribs (£3.95), Rowter medieval chicken with raisins, almonds and red wine (£7.80), and a creamy tagliatelle with Stilton, walnuts and mushrooms (£5.20). Puddings may be equally exotic; times are 12-2 and 7-9pm.

Telephone: 0629 650302.

# Youlgreave to Over Haddon

~ Approximately 6 miles ~

*A well-marked, though fairly demanding walk with some very rewarding views, taking you through a section of the Derbyshire Dales National Nature Reserve, where there is a diversity of flora and fauna to be found. Special care should always be taken near mining remains.*

**Parking**

OS Map 119 Ref SK9164. Car park at Moor Lane picnic site.

From the car park continue along the lane past the picnic site. After a 5-minute walk you reach a farm gate and stile with a public footpath sign on your left. Cross the stile to traverse a field, passing old calcite workings before reaching a minor road. Cross over and your route is waymarked (ignore the numbers on some of the waymarkers; they refer to another series of paths) and well defined, descending gently across three fields to Meadow Place Grange. Go straight across the farmyard then pass between farm buildings to a footpath straight ahead bearing slightly right. At a field gate join a track and drop down into Lathkill Dale. Cross the river and climb up steeply to the village of Over Haddon. Bear right at the public car park and continue to the far end of the village to the pub.

# Lathkil (Free House)

 This busy and friendly pub has stunning views over the dale and over miles of beautiful Derbyshire countryside. There are low ceilings with oak beams, a small well kept bar with an open fireplace, and a restaurant where children are welcome at lunchtime and which has a no-smoking area.

On draught: Wards Sheffield Best, Mild and Thorne Best, Tuborg. Food: generous portions of home-made dishes may include lasagne (£4.25), smoked trout fillet (£5.10), and lamb curry (£3.70), all served with chips and peas or a salad. For a smaller snack, try the cheese or meat cobs (rolls) with salad garnish (from £1.70). Puddings may include walnut flan, chocolate mousse and, of course, Bakewell pudding; times are 12-2pm and 7-9pm.

Telephone: 0629 812501.

**R**etrace your steps to the bottom of the dale, and turn right through a gate at the house. Walk along the dale and through a second gate into the National Nature Reserve. Follow the path along the river for just over a mile, cross an old wooden bridge and you are now in Cales Dale. Continue as far as a fork in the path, take the left fork downhill to a stile at the bottom of the hill, and then climb up the steep, stepped path on the other side. At the top, pass through the gate and head towards another gate through the field. After a third gate, follow the footpath up past Calling Low Farm on your right, and continue, keeping the road to your right. At the corner of the field, head away from the road, over a stile and into a small copse. On emerging from the copse, follow the well-established footpath through the barley field and over a stile towards some road signs ahead. Cross another stile and turn left along the road to arrive back at your car.

**Further Exploration**

Over Haddon is a beautiful hill-top village of limestone buildings, whose pretty church of St Anne is well worth a visit.

**Lathkill Dale Craft Centre**

It is in the village and has a number of individual workshops including stained glass, carpentry, lace-making, clock-making, and others. All workshops offer articles for sale. Open 10am - 5pm.

**Lathkill Dale Lead Mining**

A number of features from the Dale's past as a source of lead remain and can be easily examined by the visitor, but do not attempt any underground exploration without expert guidance. The Peak District Mining Museum at Matlock Bath has extensive displays, public areas and information about lead mining in Derbyshire.
Telephone: 0629 583834.

# Rowthorne to Hardwick Hall

〜 Approximately 5 miles 〜

*An easy, straightforward walk, taking in a mixture of open arable farmland, woods and, for much of the way, parts of Hardwick Park surrounding Hardwick Hall. For some, the views will be spoilt by the sound of the M1.*

**Parking**

OS Map 120 Ref 476647. Car park and picnic site just south of Rowthorne village.

**Further Exploration**

Hardwick Hall

This spectacular Elizabethan house, now owned by the National Trust, was built in 1591 for Bess of Hardwick, after the death of her fourth husband, the Earl of Shrewsbury. There are numerous tapestries with some by Mary, Queen of Scots who was the Earl of Shrewsbury's prisoner for 15 years. Walled courtyards enclose fine gardens. Telephone: 0246 850430.

Turn right out of the car park and go up through the village. Just before the Old School on the right, take the footpath to the left. Go straight ahead, crossing two fields and a minor road. Cross over the next field and a stile in the right corner, head for an obvious 'elbow' in the road and approach Ault Hucknall. Immediately past the church, take the bridleway off to the left. Pass a stone-built house (1724) on the right and leave the track to pass through a gate on the left. Bear right down Broad Oak Hill, following the line of the fence but keeping 50 yards to its left. Crossing a tarmac road, go through the gate in the fence opposite and continue down the hill to the far corner of the park, with some pools to your left. A gate in the the corner will give access to a bridle path, passing a quarry, to arrive at a small car park with toilets and an information board relating to the Park. Backtrack for a short distance and take the path to the right with Great Pond ahead. Bear right round the lake and head up towards the motorway. On reaching a road, turn left and left again following a signpost to Hardwick Hall. The pub is ahead of you on the right-hand side of the entrance to the Park.

# Hardwick Inn (Free House)

A traditional, beautifully proportioned building of the early 17th century, set on the edge of Hardwick Park, has numerous original outbuildings and a large lawned garden. It contains two bars, two rooms where bar food is served, two family rooms, and a Carvery restaurant. It is warmed by coal fires, and is very comfortable and popular at all times. Visitors might be interested to read of the inn's 400-year history, retold in a book by a local resident. No dogs.

On draught: Younger Scotch, Theakston XB, McEwan, Guinness, Autumn Gold and Dry Blackthorn ciders. Food: servings are ample and mouthwatering. Bar meals include dishes like T-bone steak (£8.70), scampi (£4.15), ploughman's (£2.80), and various vegetarian dishes (from £3.85). A children's menu is also available. In the Carvery (closed Mon), a fixed-price, 3-course meal costs £8.85 and there is also a carte; times are 11.30-2pm and 6.30-9.30pm. Booking is advisable for the carvery, which can get very busy.

Telephone: 0246 850245.

**Bolsover Castle, Bolsover**
Bess of Hardwick's son rebuilt this Norman castle in 1613. There are pseudo-Gothic vaulted ceilings, fine fireplaces, and ornate panelling. Be sure to see the elaborately painted ceilings of the 'star chamber', the Elysium room and the Heaven room.
Telephone: 0246 823349.

Higham, to the west, is a 17th-century street village and a conservation area. Ogston reservoir is nearby.

Sherwood Forest and the Dukeries are to the east, including Clumber Park, Thoresby Park and Welbeck Abbey.

Turn right out of the pub and follow the road uphill. At a sharp bend, leave the road and go through a gate on the right, cutting up to the left-hand corner of this field and a stile. At the top of a short incline, turn right and almost immediately left into a wood. Through a gate out of the wood, turn left past Norwood Holiday Cottages. At Norwood Lodge, take the path to the left, walk along a private drive and straight across a field, aiming for a wood on the far side. On the far side of the wood, cross a footbridge and stile, and in the next field, head for the left-hand corner. You are now on an old railway line and have a choice of paths. You can continue over the line and go straight ahead over four fields to reach a lane. Turn left here and left again at a road, to the car park. However, if this path is too muddy, turn left along the railway line and this too will take you back to your car.

# Alsop-en-le-Dale to Alstonefield

~ Approximately 6 miles ~

*Quite a strenuous walk through classic limestone scenery, with some steep gradients, passing through part of Dove Dale and several lesser known dales. Good footwear to cope with stony and sometimes muddy conditions is required.*

**Parking**

OS Map 119 SK 1554 Alsop-en-le-Dale car park on the A515 (charge 30p).

**Further Exploration**
Haddon Hall
Set in beautiful gardens, this is a perfect example of a medieval manor house, trapped in time and hardly changed for 400 years. The oldest parts - the painted chapel, the kitchen, and the banqueting hall with its minstrels' gallery - date from the 14th century.
Telephone: 0629 812855.

From the car park cross the main road to a footpath signed 'Dove Dale and Nab's Dale'. Bear diagonally across a field, over a minor road onto a farm road signed 'New Hanson Grange'. Fork left before the farm buildings and climb steadily. At a footpath fingerpost keep ahead, dropping down towards the Grange. A waymarked path bypasses farm buildings, returning to the main track at a farm gate. Turn right at a footpath sign and shortly enter Nab's Dale (NT). Dove Dale soon opens up in front of you and here follow the newly constructed path left, downstream. Almost immediately, pass Dove Holes - a famous cave system. Continue gently downhill to a footbridge over the river. Cross it, turn right and soon negotiate a squeeze wall stile, turning left into Hall Dale. Climb up the valley, with scree slopes above, to a stile, then at the head of the Dale proceed ahead towards a group of buildings. At the farm track turn left and at the end, turn right into the village of Stanshope. Follow the lane, passing Stanshope Hall and Grove Farm, the metalled surface deteriorating into a rough track down to a road. Cross and follow the path uphill, alongside the wall to the top. On reaching a gap in the wall, take the path diagonally across the field, towards a stile in the far wall (to the left of the church). Follow the line of fence, cross a stile on the right and shortly follow a walled path to the road. Turn left for the pub.

# The George (Burtonwood)

This stone-built, 250-year-old pub stands beside the village green. The decor is simple, but the atmosphere is happy and comfortable and it is significant that the proprietors have been here for around 30 years. There is one bar with two or three sitting areas and also a large dining room with long tables. In fine weather customers can sit outside and children are welcome here and in the dining room. Dogs, however, are not permitted.

On draught: Burtonwood Bitter and mild, James Forshaw Premium, Guinness, Skol, Strongbow cider. Food: generous portions of good old favourites are served, for example, meat and potato pie, chicken and chips, various types of ploughman's, sandwiches, quiche, smoked trout and for pudding, perhaps, an apple Bakewell; times are 12-2pm and 7-10pm.

Telephone: 033527 205.

On leaving the pub retrace your steps for a little way, continue past the church and shortly take a well defined footpath on the right. Head diagonally across the field. Dove Dale soon comes into view again, and then the path descends very steeply into Milldale. If you are daunted by this slope, return to the lane, turn right and proceed to Milldale this easier way. In Milldale cross the famous 'Viators' footbridge. The path now lies directly ahead up the very steep hill - an alternative way is to follow the river downstream until you reach Nab's Dale and then retrace your steps of the earlier part of the walk. Zig-zag your way uphill to a marker post, do not follow the yellow arrow, but go straight ahead through a squeeze stile. Follow the right-hand wall through three fields to a road. Turn left and retrace your steps to the right of New Hanson Grange, cross the minor road and a field to the A515 and finish up opposite the car park.

## Chatsworth House

The palatial home of the Duke and Duchess of Devonshire has one of the richest collections of fine and decorative arts in private hands. Magnificent pictures, furniture and porcelain. The enormous park is one of the finest works of landscape gardening laid out by Capability Brown. Telephone: 0246 582204.

## Arbor Low

This early Bronze Age henge monument, the largest stone circle in the Peak, is a short walk from a farm on the unclassified road leading from the A515 at Parsley Hay to Youlgreave. Although, unlike Stonehenge, all the stones are recumbent, the site is full of atmosphere.

# Grindon to Butterton

~ Approximately 6½ miles ~

*This walk is not too arduous although, like many valley areas, stream crossings on stepping stones can be affected dramatically by heavy rain.*

**Parking**

OS Map 119 SK0854. Grindon village church.

**Further Exploration**

The crags seen from the early part of this walk are above the Manifold Valley and its Thors Cave, both in reach of Grindon. That particular valley is well worth a visit, you could even hire cycles at Waterhouses on the A523 so that you could cover more distance.

Walk back towards the village but keep left past the church gate - you can cross the children's playground to achieve this. Descend the lane and turn left at the footpath sign. Continue down the field, over a brook, up into the next field, and over an unusual stile. Cross the road and another stile, then descend by a well-defined path into the valley bottom to a sign which indicates you are at the base of Ossoms Hill. Cross the footbridge, over a stile and immediately turn left and over another stile into Hoo Brook Valley which you follow for quarter of a mile on its right side before crossing a stile and stepping stones to continue with the valley on its left side. At some cottages, cross a stile, then the brook again, and follow the road to the end, crossing a ford onto the footpath on the other side. Turn right up this path and cross footbridges to save getting wet feet, as this is both a road and stream bed. Climb up the quite steep hill and, shortly after passing the Manifold Arts and Craft Centre, bear right into a very narrow lane up to Butterton Church and the pub.

# Black Lion Inn (Free House)

This welcoming, traditional village inn has a good reputation locally for both its food and beer. An ale house since 1782, it still retains a wealth of old beams and uneven floors that give it such character. There is a country dining room open on Friday and Saturday nights, and for Sunday lunch. Children are welcome.

On draught: Theakston Best and Old Peculier, Younger No 3, McEwan 70/-, Scotch and Mild, Guinness, Becks, Taunton's Blackthorn and Autumn Gold ciders. Food: daily specials may include dishes such as broccoli and cheese pie (£4.25), chicken curry or lasagne verde (both £4.45), liver and onions, and ploughman's with four different cheeses (£3.50); times are 12-2pm (closed Wed lunch) and 7-9pm.

Telephone: 0538 304232.

Turn left, then left again at the end of the car park, signposted to Onecote and Warslow. Just as the road starts to climb out of a dip, turn left onto a track and pass the front of Greenlow Head House, keeping left by the stone wall. Over a stile, walk through a narrow field and into another which descends towards the valley bottom. Before you reach the corner of a wall, turn right towards a stile in a wall at the other side of the field. Keep on this clear footpath, through many stiles to a brook just beyond a tiny cottage. Keep to the right of the barn and head straight up the hill, past another farm, to the main road. Turn left and in about quarter of a mile, turn right onto a track, immediately turning left and passing through a gate. Keep left, walk over a cattle grid, and at the next gate, turn left and continue beside a fence, then a wall. Just after a long line of duckboards, cross a stile then squeeze through the wall, turning left to follow this wall to another stile. Keep left of the farm, and stiles will take you over the farm track, heading towards Grindon church, to the road. Cross, and follow the fingerpost over the next wall. The path is fairly obvious and heads back directly to the church.

# Beeston to Higher Burwardsley

~ Approximately 6½ miles ~

*A pleasant walk between the historic fortresses of Beeston Castle and Peckforton Castle through fields and woods with some steep uphill stretches*

**Parking**

OS Map 117 Ref SJ 5359. Picnic area below Beeston Castle (follow signs for the castle in the village; the picnic site is on the left just below the entrance ).

**Further Exploration**

**Beeston Castle**

There are spectacular views from the impressive ruins of this stronghold built on an inaccessible crag by the Earl of Chester in the 13th century and now in the care of English Heritage.

**Cholondeley Castle Gardens**

Lovely ornamental gardens, with woodland and lakeside walks, rare breeds of farm animals and a lakeside picnic area, are open on Sun and BHs from Easter to September.

Telephone 0829 720383

From the picnic site walk back to the village, turn left down the main road, past a phone box, then shortly take the right fork, signed Bunbury. Pass two farmhouses and at the left bend, take the Peckforton footpath sign on the right over a stile onto a farm track (it can be muddy). Go left up the track, past a small wood and where the track peters out into fields, take the stile on your right (yellow arrow) into the field, cross to and skirt the edge of the wood. At the end of the wood, cross the field, keeping fairly close to a small lake on your left, to reach a stile in the far corner on to the road opposite the Gothic stone gateway of Peckforton Castle. Turn left up the road, and keep on to a stile, right, waymarked 'Sandstone Trail, Burwardsley', and cross into the field to walk steeply uphill following a well defined path (yellow arrows). Almost at the crest, below a house, take the stile, left, to cross a neck of field to a stile opposite onto a path between the field edge and a belt of trees. This joins a lane leading down to a cobbled lane. Here turn right uphill, and stay with the lane all the way over the top of the hill, and down to a T junction, where you turn right and right again, opposite a telephone box, for the pub.

On leaving the pub, turn right and carry on down the very quiet lane which ends at a gate into estate woodland. Go through (nature conservancy area, dogs on lead and no bikes) and keep to the broad, well sheltered path that winds along the bottom of the wooded hillside to emerge onto a road with Beeston Castle opposite across the fields. Turn right up the road, ignore the first marked footpath left, but take the second, hugging the field edge across the first field down to two stiles and some steps up into the second field and head along a well defined path towards a bungalow. Cross the road to a stile opposite into a wood (signed Beacon Hill), and follow the path round and up through the trees to join a narrow track leading alongside a stone wall to emerge at the side of the picnic area.

# Pheasant (Bass)

This is a delightful small country pub, tucked away in the depths of the country in the Peckforton Hills about halfway along the Sandstone Trail. Its outbuildings have been converted to provide comfortable well equipped bedroom accommodation, but the pub itself, built of brick and timber, has not lost its friendly, traditional atmosphere. Its old, low-beamed rooms have been made into one comfortable bar with an open log fire at its centre.

On draught: Draught Bass and Bass Mild, Worthington Best Bitter, Stones Bitter, Guinness, Carling Black Label and Dry Blackthorn cider. Food: the menu, with a leaning towards seafood, might include avocado and smoked trout salad or hot avocado with prawns, cod, plaice and herbs, both at £3.20, terrine of duck and local pheasant at £2.30, pork in cider at £4.95 or fish and egg pie at £4.50; times are 12.15-2pm and 7.15-9 or 9.30pm. There is also a restaurant, open evenings only, and in summer a conservatory and small, attractive garden.

Telephone: 0829 70434

# Park Gate to Lower Peover

~ Approximately 6 miles ~

*A pleasant walk through Cheshire's fields and lanes, using footpaths across part of the landscaped grounds of Peover Hall.*

### Parking

OS Map 118 Ref SJ7874. By Park Gate village hall

### Further Exploration

St Oswald's Church

Its churchyard adjoining the pub, the church is a black and white timbered building with a stone tower. It is famous for its ancient and massive oak dug-out chest. By tradition, any girl aspiring to marry a local farmer has to be strong enough to fling back its lid with one hand.

From the village hall head up the lane away from the main road to turn left into a broad, tree-lined grassy avenue leading to a meadow in front of Peover Hall. Cross a low fence and go through a gate into the meadow, crossing to a stile opposite, to the right of the hall. Cross the lane, following footpath signs, then turn right into the stableyard and follow signs across the yard towards St Lawrence's Church. Skirt the church wall, go along the pleached path leading into a copse and follow the marked path to a stile. Cross the field to another stile, cross, turn right and go down the field side, with the fence on your right, to a third stile. Cross, turn left down the hill to the main drive through the park, near the lake. Cross over the cattle grid and continue to the lodge gates and the main road. Cross the busy A50, and walk up a few yards to your right to the waymarked bridleway and farm lane on your left that leads you past a right fork and through a farmyard to a gate. Keep straight on to another farm, shortly after which you emerge at the entrance to Freegreen Farm. At Freegreen Lane, turn right and continue for about a mile, and take the left turn just past the post office, then left again down a cul-de-sac and across a stream. You will then see a sign to the pub on your right.

# Bells of Peover (Greenall Whitney)

The white-painted walls of this charming old pub, which looks out across its patio onto the church, are covered with wisteria and there are tables outside in summer. Inside is a series of attractive, traditionally furnished rooms, some small, some large, with a fine collection of Toby jugs. Children under 14 are not allowed in the bar, though welcome at the tables outside or in the restaurant.

On draught: Greenalls Bitter, Original and Mild, Guinness, Carling Black Label, Labatt's, and a good selection of wines. Food: the menu ranges from sandwiches (from £1.75) and filled potatoes (from £3.45) to substantial dishes like steak and kidney pie (£4.75) or lasagne (£4.60); times are 12-2pm and 6.30-8.30pm Mon-Fri. There is also an à la carte restaurant open 7-9.30pm Wed-Sat and also Sun lunch.

Telephone: 0565 722269.

On leaving the pub, retrace your steps to Freegreen Lane and turn right, continuing to Fox Covert Lane (beside Well Cottage) where you turn right. Follow this lane until you come to a small lane on your left, and follow this until it rejoins Freegreen Lane. Turn right and continue until you come to the A50. Cross over (with care) and walk up to your left, shortly reaching Long Lane on your right. This leads past farms and some glasshouses, then becomes a bridleway skirting the grounds of Peover Hall. Go through a gate by St Anthony's Cottages into the lane, and continue until you see the stable buildings of Peover Hall on your left. Turn left here, retracing your steps to cross the lane and the stile back into the meadow for the return to Park Gate.

# Bickley Moss to Cholmondeley

➣ Approximately 6 miles ➣

*A walk on quiet country lanes through the pastoral landscape of the Cheshire plain near Cholmondeley Castle.*

**Parking**

OS Map 117 Ref SJ5349. Near the church.

**Further Exploration**

Cholmondeley Castle

The grounds and gardens, immediately opposite the pub on the other side of the main road, are open Sun and BHs from 4 April to 17 October.

Telephone: 0829 720383.

Leaving the church on your left, head down to the T-junction, and turn left towards the A49, which you cross (with care) into the lane opposite. Take the first turning left into a lane that winds past Norbury Common to a crossroads. Here, turn left and continue to another crossroads, turning left again. At Chorley Bank, a sharp left-hand bend brings you to what looks like a village school, standing on your right, a little way back from the junction with the main road.

## Cholmondeley Arms (Whitbread)

This most unusual pub was a village school until its transfomration in the 1980s. The interior retains its character, the large, high-ceilinged, interconnecting school rooms forming a T-shape with the bar at the centre and a gallery above.

On draught: Marston's Pedigree, Flowers IPA, Boddingtons, guest beers, Stella Artois, Heineken, Heineken Export, Murphy's, and Strongbow cider. Food: a large range of imaginative specials, priced from about £5 to £9, might include braised beef with ginger, salmon and spinach lasagne, or crisply fried whitebait. Home-made soups, ploughman's, salads, sandwiches and a children's menu are also available; times are 12-2.15pm, 6.30-10pm. There are 4 bedrooms for guests.

Telephone: 0829 720300.

Turn right out of the yard to come to the A49, and cross over carefully, into the lane skirting the beautiful wooded grounds of Cholmondeley Castle. You will pass a track on the left leading to Red Hall, but continue to the next turning on your left and follow this lane down, going straight over the crossroads until you come to a T-junction where a left turn brings you back to Bickley Church.

# Keld to Muker

~ Approximately 5 miles ~

Walk into the small square and take the arrowed footpath in the north-east corner. At a junction of paths, keep straight on, pass through a gate and climb uphill. Follow the Pennine Way signs up to a gap in a wall and along the edge of Kisdon Hill. Cross numerous wall stiles eventually going downhill towards a derelict house. Leave the Pennine Way here and follow a steep lane downhill into the village of Muker.

## Farmers Arms (Free House)

This welcoming pub is truly a farmers' local. The L-shaped bar, has comfortable cushioned wall-seats and pine tables, and a small shelf near the entrance offers visitors some books to read and leaflets on local attractions. Outside, there are tables on the front terrace. Children are welcome.

On draught: Theakston Old Peculier, Best and XB, Butterknowle Bitter, Harp, McEwans. Food: popular pub food is good value and includes filled baps (£1.25), toasted sandwiches (£1.50), omelettes (£3.25), lasagne (£3.50),filled jacket potatoes (£1.90), steak pie (£3.50) and soup (£1); times are 12-3pm and 7-9pm.

Telephone: 0748 86297.

Walk back through the village,then follow the footpath waymarked 'Gunnerside and Keld'. Cross a stile, and follow the established path across meadows. Cross a footbridge over the Swale, bear left and follow the track beside the river. After a mile, at Swinner Gill, pass through a gate and climb the steep track leading to the remains of Crackpot Hall - a short diversion to the right. Keep to the path, then later, fork left downhill passing East Gill Force on the left, and cross a wooden bridge over the Swale. Follow the path uphill to join your outward route back to Keld square.

*This is a delightful ramble through Upper Swaledale affording views of upland moorland and the green fields of the Swale valley.*

**Parking**
OS Maps 92 & 98 Ref NY8901. Keld village.

**Further Exploration**
Muker is the largest of a trio of delightful villages near the head of Swaledale. Situated at the foot of Kisdon Hill are grey stone cottages, an Elizabethan church, a chapel and an Institute - all additions to the village during the lead-mining days, remains of which are evident on the hillside. Pioneer botanists Cherry and Richard Kearton, who were the first to use photographs for illustrating botanical books, went to school here and are commemorated in the chapel. The Pennine Way, coming in from Kisdon Hill and part of this walk, follows the old 'Corpse Way' - the route coffin-bearers used from Muker to the church at Grinton, before their own village church was built.

# Glaisdale to Egton Bridge

∽ Approximately 5 miles ∽

*Not a long walk but a fairly robust one with some short bursts of lung-stretching climbing through the delightful wooded Esk Valley.*

**Parking**

OS Map 94 Ref NZ7705. Underneath the railway arches by Glaisdale Station.

**Further Exploration**

Glaisdale

One of the bridges which span the River Esk is the tiny Beggars Bridge, built in 1619 by Tom Ferris, a local boy made good, as a gesture to prove his worth to the doubting father of the Egton girl he courted.

The road climbs up from the railway to Glaisdale village. To your left is a track marked 'Unsuitable for Motors'. Turn up here, ignoring the footpath signposted 'coast to coast footpath'. The stony track climbs steeply uphill to the left passing a cottage on the right. When the main track carries on through a gate, follow the clear path that veers off, still steeply, to the left. As the incline lessens, ignore the footpath to the left which goes over a wooden wall stile, but bear right and keep climbing steadily. After about quarter of a mile, a National Park footpath sign marks a clear track to your left. Follow the sign through the gate along the track until you reach the unclassified road from Rosedale to Egton Bridge. Turn left and follow the road downhill for about three-quarters of a mile to the ford where salmon can be seen crossing the road when the river is running high. Round the corner from the ford is the Horseshoe

# Horseshoe Hotel (Free House)

Picturesquely situated on the banks of the River Esk, this charming pub has a large and well-kept garden and its own island in the middle of the River Esk, which is sometimes open to the public. Inside there is an unspoilt, comfortable 'L'-shaped bar, in part of which children are allowed. Like all pubs in this beautiful area, it gets very busy in the summer but service is always brisk and efficient. There is overnight accommodation.

On draught: Theakston Best, XB and Old Peculier, Tetley Bitter and a guest beer. Food: the home-cooked meals are good quality and served in generous portions, Yorkshire style. Typical dishes include steak and kidney pie (£5.25), steak (from £8.50) and freshly cut sandwiches (from £1.95); times are 12-2pm and 6.45-9pm and there is also a separate restaurant with an à la carte menu.

Telephone: (0947) 85245.

**Egton Bridge**
This is one of England's most famous Roman Catholic parishes, known as 'the village missed by the Reformation'. It is the birthplace of Father Nicholas Postgate, 'Martyr of the Moors' who kept the faith alive when Roman Catholics were persecuted. He was executed in York, aged 82, for baptising a child into the Catholic faith in 1679.

Walk up the left-hand drive towards the road, immediately turning left down the short path that leads to the River Esk. Cross the two sets of stepping stones and follow the path onto the road which runs on the far bank of the river. At the road, turn left and follow the road and river under the railway bridge, up the hill, to a footpath sign on your left pointing over a stile. Follow this path, keeping the fence to your left, to the beck where there is a footpath sign on a tree. Cross the field as indicated up a very steep, but mercifully short slope and cross the stile at the end of the conifer wood. Follow the steep path through the wood and over another stile, keeping the hedge to your left at all times. Over the next stile, follow the track past the television mast, and you will see a farmyard in front of you. Do not follow the path right through the farmyard, but veer left by the water-trough to the gate, and then turn right onto the road. This is Limber Hill. Turn left and follow the road as it drops down to the River Esk again and then back to your starting point beneath the railway arches at Glaisdale.

# Malham Tarn to Malham

∽ Approximately 6 miles ∽

*A beautiful walk through some of the finest limestone scenery in Britain. The view from the top of the Cove is magnificent - a panorama down the Aire valley into the southern dales. Take care on the loose stones which can be very treacherous when wet.*

**Parking**

OS Map 98 Ref SD8965. Malham Tarn car park.

**Further Exploration**

Malham Tarn

Unique in Britain in being the only upland, lime-rich lake of any significant size, the tarn measures 1km across but only 5 metres deep at the most. Generally, water will sink through the porous limestone but the tarn is on impermeable slate, and is surrounded by limestone rocks which give it its lime-rich character. It is a haven for lime-loving plants and wintering duck.

Turn right from the car park onto the road and cross a stream, taking the path on the left (waymarked) through a gate. Follow this grassy path, keeping left, heading downstream until you reach a fork in the path. Bear left towards Water Sinks and Malham Cove on the path winding downhill, eventually bearing left over a stile and down the middle of the Watlowes valley. Bear right with the path onto the rock 'pavement' on top of Malham Cove, and cross it (with care), climb over a ladder stile, descend the steps into the cove, and follow the stream to the foot of the cove wall. Follow this established path to a road. Bear left and remain on this road into the village of Malham. To find the pub, turn left over a footbridge.

## Lister Arms (Free House)

This large stone-built pub sits in a beautiful location, close to the stream which flows through the village. Inside, the main bar is warm and welcoming with two open fires burning in large stone fireplaces. There is plenty of comfortable seating in the carpeted bar, and a second room houses a pool table. There is also a garden.

On draught: Younger Scotch, Burton Ale, Guinness and at least three guest beers. Food: the lunchtime menu offers good hearty meals, for example, steak and Guinness pie (£4.95), sandwiches from (£1.75) and ploughman's (£3.50). There is also a separate children's menu; times are 12-2pm and 7.30-9pm (restaurant 9.30pm). No food on Monday, except in summer; booking essential on Saturday evenings.

Telephone: 0729 830330.

Return across the bridge and bear left, ignore the road bridge and shortly cross back over the stream, and take the path waymarked 'Pennine Way' over a stile, following Malham Beck downstream. At a kissing gate, take the path following the wall on the left away from the Pennine Way towards a barn. Keep to the footpath, crossing a stile, now following Gordale Beck. Enter National Trust woodland, and the path eventually reaches Janet's Foss - a small, 16ft-high waterfall. Legend has it that the cave it guards was the home of Jenet, the queen of the local fairies. When the path joins a lane, bear right and walk to Gordale Bridge. Take the path arrowed 'Malham Cove' on the left. Follow the yellow markers uphill through gates and over stiles, passing through a field containing signs of several Iron-Age hut circles and enclosures before reaching a lane. Turn right and follow the lane uphill before crossing a stile and following the path arrowed to the left. Follow this grassy path across the scarred limestone landscape and moorland. Keep bearing left and join the Pennine Way, cross a stile to return to the road and the car park.

### Malham Cove

This is one of England's great natural wonders, with its 70 metre high sheer walls. It was formed by the combined erosional effects of both ice and water on the weak Craven Fault some 12,000 years ago, when meltwater would have flowed down the Watlowes valley, then over the cliff as a waterfall; glaciers, too, flowed over the cliff at some stage. The result is the beautiful, yet striking wide cove with Malham Beck flowing out from the base of the cliff.

Before reaching the path to Water Sinks and Malham Cove at the beginning of your walk, on your right about 1km away is a chimney which is the remains of a smelt mill used in the 19th century to smelt local lead, ore and zinc ore.

A good diversion from the main route is to follow the path waymarked to Gordale Scar. Follow the stream into a dramatic and beautiful gorge down which cascades animpressive double waterfall which can be climbed (with care) when not in spate.

# Flasby to Hetton

⮑ Approximately 4 miles ⮐

*A peaceful ramble along the Flasby and Hetton becks and the moorland flanks of Flasby Fell.*

**Parking**

OS Map 103 Ref SD9456.In the hamlet of Flasby

Head downhill towards a farm and take the path on the left waymarked to Hetton. Follow the path along the banks of the small beck, through gates and fields. When you see fingerposts pointing away from the beck, follow these across fields to join a road, and bear right into Hetton. The pub lies on left at the far end of village.

## Angel (Free House)

This elegant stone-built pub has four attractively decorated rooms where a warm welcome awaits, especially in winter beside the log fires, or solid-fuel stove; the main bar has a farmhouse range in its stone fireplace. Pictures and photographs adorn the walls, and fresh flowers add a splash of colour. Children are welcome in the eating area and restaurant.

On draught: Theakston Bitter and XB, Timothy Taylor Landlord, Tetley, Guinness, Carlsberg, Beck's. There is also a good wine list. Food: good value for money, the menu offers dishes like Provençale fish soup (£2.70), local goat's cheese baked in filo pastry, with green salad (£4.85), salmon with cucumber and dill (£6.50), and spinach noodles with garlic and basil sauce (£3.85). Open sandwiches (from £4.95) are available at lunchtime. Puddings may include crème brûlée and summer pudding (from £2.75); times are 12-2pm (2.30pm Sun) and 6-10pm (not Sun).

Telephone: 0756 730263.

**R**eturn along the road to a footpath on the left, signposted Rylstone. Follow this to a house on the left with a large picture window, and take the wall stile on the right, crossing a field and passing through two gates to cross the railway. Head towards and pass to the right of a barn, then behind the barn pass through the gate immediately ahead. Continue straight on through a further gate, turn right through a third gate and cross the field to a stone stile. Over the stile, bear diagonally left across the field and follow the track under the railway, towards a stone wall. Cross the ladder stile and go directly uphill to a gate into a small copse and on towards another gate. Through this, head down to and through (yellow arrows) a farm, then follow the Flasby fingerpost. Shortly, bear right off the track, through two gates and across the meadow to another gate and a fingerpost. Follow this footpath downhill into a farmyard and on to Flasby.

# Barden Bridge to Appletreewick

∾ Approximately 5½ miles ∾

*A beautiful and peaceful walk along the River Wharfe through outstanding scenery. Birdlife to look out for includes herons and kestrels, dippers and wagtails*

**Parking**

OS Maps 98,99 & 104 Ref SE0557. Parking area near Barden Bridge.

**Further Exploration**

Barden Tower

Located over the gracefully arched Barden Bridge and uphill on the B road, the tower is a ruined 3-storey hunting lodge overlooking the River Wharfe.

Bolton Abbey

The romantic ruins stand in parkland on the river bank 3 miles south of Barden Bridge. The abbey was founded by Augustinian canons in 1151 and the nave survives in use to this day as a parish church.

Parcevall Hall Gardens, Skyreholme, near Appletreewick

In a beautiful hillside setting, east of the main Wharfedale valley, the gardens of this Elizabethan house are open daily. Telephone 0756 720311.

Follow the lane away from the bridge for a short distance before taking a footpath signposted to Howgill. This well-established path, the Dales Way, follows the River Wharfe upstream for nearly two miles. Soon after a long flight of steps, and where the river flows round an island, there is a campsite beside the river, and here you bear right onto the path signposted to Appletreewick. When you join a road, turn right and follow it uphill to the pub.

## Craven Arms (Free House)

This fine pub has two small bars with open fires, and one even has an old black kitchen range. Beamed ceilings, stone walls, attractive settles and carved chairs combine to create a cosy, welcoming atmosphere. Hundreds of bank notes adorn the ceiling, while old agricultural tools, copper pans and brassware are dotted around the rooms. Outside, there are plenty of bench seats on which to admire the outstanding views. Children are welcome.

On draught: Theakston Best, XB and Old Peculier, Younger Scotch, Guinness. Food: generous portions offer good value and dishes may include vegetable and pasta bake (£4), steak and kidney pie (£3.75), and local pork sausage, jacket potato and salad (£3.50); times are 12-2pm and 7-9pm (9.30pm at weekends).

Telephone: 0756 720270.

Follow the lane through Appletreewick and take the second turning right towards Skyreholme. In a short distance, take the waymarked footpath on your right through a farmyard, and bear right through a gate. Pass a campsite on the left and cross two stiles, following a path overlooking a beck, downhill to join a lane. Bear left, cross a bridge and rejoin the Dales Way along the river bank back to Barden Bridge.

# Buckden to Hubberholme
 ∽ Approximately 4½ miles ∽

Walk down to a small green by the post office. Cross the green and follow a lane over a bridge, then take the footpath (Dales Way) on the right and follow it beside the River Wharfe, signposted to Hubberholme. When you reach a lane, turn right into the quiet hamlet of Hubberholme. The pub is on the left by the bridge.

*An idyllic ramble along lush meadowland paths and upland tracks with fine views of Upper Wharfedale's glacial valley and hillsides and of Langstrothdale. Look out for river birds, specially dippers and grey wagtails.*

## George Inn (Free House)

This remote and unspoilt pub in a peaceful hamlet offers a relaxing break and a friendly welcome. The bar is quite small and has burnished copper-topped tables, stone walls, flagstone floors, beams and a large warming fireplace with a wood-burning stove. A second bar also offers comfortable seating and has stone walls adorned with numerous prints. Good seating on the terrace catches the sun and faces the moors. Children are welcome in the room next to the bar.

On draught: Younger No 3 and Scotch, Harp, Beck's. Food: although short, the menu offers good-value, hearty food including large crusty rolls filled with cheese, ham, tuna or beef (£2.40), home-made soup (£1.35), steak and kidney pie (£4.40), and ploughman's (£2.65); times are 12-2pm and 7-8.45pm.

Telephone: 0756 760223.

Cross the bridge towards the church and take the footpath adjacent to the churchyard waymarked 'Scar House & Yockenthwaite' and follow this uphill. Pass behind Scar House and, at a fingerpost, take the path waymarked to Cray, along the edge of the wood. Keep following yellow markers on rocks and posts and pass through a farmyard down into Cray. Cross the road and stream near the White Lion and follow the path uphill waymarked 'Buckden'. Keep to this track through fields and gates below Buckden Pike to the car park.

**Parking**
OS Map 98 Ref SD9477.
Buckden car park.

**Further Exploration**
Hubberholme
Of particular interest is its church, St Michael and all Angels, which originated as a forest chapel. It is probably the best-loved of all Dales churches, with a superb riverside setting against a backcloth of wooded hillside and distant bare fells. Hunt for woodwork inside by the Yorkshire woodcarver Robert Thompson, which can be identified by his 'signature' - delightful carved mice hidden away in unsuspected places. The ashes of the author J.B. Priestley, are scattered nearby and a plaque dedicated to him is in the church.

# Pateley Bridge to Wath-in-Nidderdale

∽ Approximately 5½ miles ∽

*This is a tranquil river walk through beautiful Nidderdale with a return route affording panoramic views of the dale and surrounding hills and moors.*

**Parking**

OS Map 99 Ref SE1565. Car park in centre of Pateley Bridge.

**Further Exploration**

Pateley Bridge and Nidderdale

In the days of water-powered mills this was the most industrialised of the major Dales, specialising in the manufacture of linen and hemp from locally grown flax. With the advent of steam power, linen-manufacture decreased and Pateley's mills turned to making cord, twine and rope and quarrying and mining were developed. Now however, agriculture and tourism are the most important activities. The history of the area is traced in the fascinating Nidderdale Museum, once a Victorian workhouse.

Take the footpath waymarked 'Wath' on the town side of the river, and head upstream. Follow a sign directing you round the back of some houses, on a path which eventually leads to the river bank. The path runs parallel to the River Nidd across meadowland, close to, and occasionally along the course of the old railway line. Eventually you will come to a quiet lane and narrow humped-back bridge. Turn right here and walk along the lane to the pub.

Return along the lane and cross the bridge. At a T-junction, cross and take the path waymarked to Heathfield and continue uphill across fields and stiles, guided by green signs with yellow arrows. Pass behind Spring Hill Farm and bear right at a quiet lane into the tiny hamlet of Heathfield. In a short distance, turn left along a track waymarked to Mosscar. Follow it uphill and at the top, follow the 'Nidderdale Way' sign through a gate into a field. Keep to the wall and follow the path through more gates, keeping the stone building to the left, eventually passing to the left of a farm. Walk downhill along a metalled drive to a quiet lane. Turn right, then left through a gate - signposted 'Nidderdale Way' - passing through a caravan site. Cross the stream, follow the track uphill, then keep left to follow a path between two stone walls, heading towards a house. Cross the brook and follow a sign, turning left into a driveway, pass in front of the house and remain on the track until you join a road. Bear left, passing the Watermill Inn - once an old flax mill, whose huge mill wheel is still working - and in a short distance, take the path on the right signed 'Pateley Bridge'. Cross the meadows on an established path to join the river bank for the return to the town and car park.

# Sportsman's Arms (Free House)

This is an old sandstone inn, set back from the road, with a well-kept garden prettily decorated with hanging flower baskets. The inn is split into lounge, dining room and bar. The comfortable, panelled bar is reached from the side of the hotel and is tastefully decorated with chintzy fabrics, carpet and smart tables. Quality prints adorn the wall. The welcome is warm and friendly to both adults and children.

On draught: Younger Scotch, McEwan Export, Guinness, Carlsberg, Beck's. Food: good-quality bar meals lean towards fish dishes - usually from nearby Whitby or local Nidd trout. The menu may include home-made soup (£2.50), fresh scallops in their shell glazed with three cheeses (£4.30), Nidderdale trout (£5.20), Scottish salmon Hollandaise (£6.25). Desserts (£2.90) include crème brûlée and their speciality, summer pudding; times are 12-2pm and 7-10pm. The restaurant is open every evening except Sunday.

Telephone: 0423 711306.

# Kilburn to Coxwold

~ Approximately 4½ miles ~

*A gentle, undemanding walk, largely through rolling farmland, with fine views of the escarpment from which the notoriously steep Sutton Bank road descends.*

**Parking**

OS Map 100 Ref SE5180. Middle of the village by the Foresters Arms.

**Further Exploration**

Kilburn

As well as being an attractive village in its own right, Kilburn is well-known for its famous White Horse, carved into the hillside in 1857 by the headmaster of the village school, assisted by pupils and villagers. It is visible for miles around, particularly on this walk.

Kilburn is also renowned as the home of Robert Thompson, a woodcarver whose furniture can be found all over the world and whose hallmark was, and still is, a small mouse which always decorates any piece of furniture or carving made by him or his successors. He died in 1955 but his grandsons have carried on the family tradition. His old home in the main village street is now a showroom for the firm's work and is open to the public.

Walk south through the village past a number of attractive cottages until, about quarter of a mile out of the village, you reach a large, rather incongruous, modern factory building. Turn left opposite this, along a footpath which becomes a little indistinct. After crossing a stile, bear left, soon to reach a track which, if you turn left, goes back into Kilburn. Turn right, heading behind the attractive barns. After passing them on your right, the footpath turns sharp left and follows a fence. Just beyond a water-trough at the end of the field, there are two stiles. Cross the one straight ahead and turn right along the hedged path to a narrow lane. Turn right here along the lane past Kilburn Thicket - rich with young pheasants and other game birds - and Fox Folly Farm. The lane eventually joins the road back to Kilburn. Opposite the right-hand turn, proceed through a white gate and bear right across the field to another white gate which brings you out almost next to Shandy Hall. The pub lies just beyond this on the left-hand side of the street.

Turn left out of the pub and immediately, there is a footpath running off the main street down to the fields behind the village. Follow this, turning left through a kissing gate after a short distance, and heading diagonally left across a field and through a second kissing gate. The path, now quite indistinct, runs diagonally right, across a field to a metal gate. Through this, follow a tree-lined path to the bottom of a hill. Bear left past a green barn, soon to reach the road just south of Fox Folly Farm. Proceed along the road for a short distance, taking the signposted bridleway across the fields to your left, which brings you out onto the Kilburn road by the entrance drive to Wildon Grange. Turn right along the Kilburn road back to the village.

## Fauconberg Arms (Free House)

 This 17th-century inn is named after the Earl of Fauconberg who lived at nearby Newburgh Hall and was married to Cromwell's daughter, Mary. There is a belief that Mary brought her father's body to the Hall after his death in 1658 and that it lies undiscovered in a bricked-up vault. There is a comfortable lounge and a bright, cheerful public bar with stone walls, huge beams, flagstone floors and a great fireplace. Children are welcome.

On draught: Theakston Best, Tetley, John Smith's, Guinness, Carlsberg. There is also an extensive wine list and no less than 10 champagnes for the better-heeled tourist. Food: the bar food ranges from soup and sandwiches (from around £2), to good hot dishes like seafood strudel (£5.95) and loin of lamb (£6.55); times are 12-2pm and 7-9pm (no bar meals Mon evening in winter). There is also a children's menu. The restaurant serves à la carte meals from about £15 a head.

Telephone: 03476 214.

### Shandy Hall

This attractive house was the home of Laurence Sterne, vicar of Coxwold in the 18th century and author of 'The Life and Opinions of Tristram Shandy, Gentleman'. Shandy Hall itself dates from the 15th and 17th centuries. It contains the largest collection anywhere of Sterne's books and manuscripts and other Sterne memorabilia. It is also open to the public. Telephone: 03476 465.

# Hutton le Hole to Lastingham

~ Approximately 5 miles ~

*A gentle, undulating walk on the southern edge of the North Yorkshire Moors, taking in two of the area's most attractive villages.*

**Parking**

OS Map 100 Ref SE7090 Public car park at the north end of the village.

**Further Exploration**

Hutton le Hole

This much-photographed village is undeniably one of the most attractive in the area, but sometimes, the sheer volume of tourists can be overwhelming. Like many parts of the National Park, it is best appreciated out of season.

The village is home to the Ryedale Folk Museum which conveys a realistic impression of rural life in this region over the last four centuries. and features cottages and buildings from neighbouring villages re-erected on site. Telephone: 07515 367.

Walk south down the main village street, past the Ryedale Folk Museum, to a gate on your left with a footpath sign. Follow the path past the bowling green and go through another gate. Follow the fence on your left, ignoring the stile on the left, then cross a stile and proceed to the corner of the field and cross another stile. Keeping the fence to your left, pass through a gate, cross the stream and follow the footpath through the wood. This brings you out onto the minor road from Hutton le Hole to Lastingham with the moors starting to rise on your left. Turn right, following the path along the grass verge. Just before the bridge over the beck, turn left over a stile and follow the path along the moor edge to Camomile Farm. Do not go through the farmyard, but bear left, and follow the wall on your right where it turns a corner. The path goes across the beck and rises to a seat overlooking Lastingham village. Turn right here, go down the path into the village, and the pub is opposite the church.

## Blacksmiths Arms (Free House)

This is an attractive, welcoming pub with a number of small, traditionally furnished rooms. It is slightly unusual for the area in that it remains open all day, even in the off season. There are seats and tables outside and a secluded beer garden at the back.

On draught: Websters Yorkshire Bitter, Bass, Stones Bitter and two guest beers. Food: bar snacks range from dishes like sweet and sour chicken (£4.25), and various curries (£4.25), to filled baguettes (£2.95) and, on most days, a traditional roast lunch, (£4.60).

Telephone: 07515 247.

Leaving the pub, turn left and follow the road towards Cropton and Pickering. After a short distance, turn right down a cul-de-sac just past Bridge Farm. The metalled road ends in a clearly defined path ahead. This climbs steeply to a wooden gate leading onto a road, where you fork left through the hamlet of Spaunton. At the T-junction at the end of the village street, turn left (No Through Road). Almost immediately, you pass through a gate which gives access to a broad and well-defined track through undulating fields. When you reach a junction of footpaths with three bridleway signs, follow the right-hand path, soon passing through two gates, keeping the line of trees on your right. In the right-hand corner of the field, pass through a further gate into Spring Wood. The path skirts the edge of the wood and then turns sharply left. As soon as you emerge from the wood, ignore the stile on your left, and keep on the tree-lined path. At a T-junction with the track to Lingmoor Farm, turn right. Keep straight on, passing a track to your left, following the track down to the river and main road at the southern end of Hutton le Hole. Turn right up the street back to the car park.

**St Mary's Church, Lastingham**
This fascinating church stands on the site of a monastery which Cedd, a monk from Lindisfarne, began to build in AD 654. Completed after his death by his brother Chad, but later destroyed in AD 866, it lay in ruins until 1078 when Stephen, Abbot of Whitby began to restore it by building a crypt as a shrine to St Cedd. Although he never completed the building, his crypt, with chancel, nave and two aisles, is a complete church within the present church, and is used for special services.

# Middleham to East Witton

~ Approximately 5 miles ~

*A delightful walk through Coverdale on defined field and river bank paths. A few short climbs with good valley views.*

**Parking**

OS Map 99 Ref SE 1287. In Middleham Square.

**Further Exploration**

**Middleham Castle**

Dominating the small town of Middleham is the 12th-century keep which saw its great days during the Wars of the Roses. The seat of the Neville family, the Earls of Warwick, it was the home for a time of Richard of Gloucester, who married the Earl's daughter Anne Neville, and later became the ill-fated King Richard III.

**Jervaulx Abbey**

Jervaulx Abbey was one of Yorkshire's great Cistercian monasteries, founded in 1156 and owning large estates, particularly in Upper Wensleydale. The picturesque and extensive ruins are open to the public and are delightfully situated in a parkland setting. They are famous as much for the wild flowers that grow all over them for their architecture.

From the square follow the road out of the town signposted Middleham Castle. When the wall on your left ends, turn left, cross through the gate and head down the field. Nearing the bottom join a grassy track and follow this down to the river. Cross the bridge and turn left, following the river until the end of the first field. Towards the end, bear right climbing a fairly steep hill. At the top go through the gate immediately ahead, then pass through another gate on the left. Bear slightly right across the field towards a small bridge over the gill (partially concealed by trees). Cross the bridge and the stile beyond and head straight across the field, keeping to the right. Maintain this direction, passing through any closed gates and a thin stile set in a wall, until you pass a small copse to your right. Go through the gate on your right. The path soon becomes a track and at a sharp right turn, cross the stile on the left, keep ahead across two more stiles and head towards the gate on the right. Beyond the gate, follow the road into the village, at the bottom of which is the pub.

## The Blue Lion (Free House)

Behind the attractive stone façade of this fine village inn is a welcoming bar decorated with unusual portraits and prints, an assortment of china, pewter, silver and dried flowers, with a large stone fireplace, flagged floors, beams and oak panelling. Benches outside at the front overlook the village green. Children are welcome. Overnight accommodation is available.

On draught: Theakston Best, XB and Old Peculier, Younger Scotch Bitter, Murphy's, Carlsberg, Beck's, Scrumpy Jack cider and a selection of fruit wines. Food: delicious home-cooked food offers dishes like wild boar terrine (£2.75), salmon in filo pastry (£7.55), roast wood pigeon with thyme, shallots and smoked bacon (£6.25) and white chocolate mousse (£3.25); times are 12-2pm and 7-9.30pm. There is a restaurant, open from Tuesday to Saturday evenings only.

Retrace your steps through the village, pass the Methodist Church and turn right through a gate. Walk up the left-hand edge of a field to a white gate, then go straight ahead over a stile and downhill to another stile, before passing through a small gate, keeping to the right. At a dilapidated barn, turn right, shortly to turn left over a stile and then go straight across the next two fields down to the bridge and road. Cross two stiles and the bridge and bear round to the left. Almost immediately after a pub, turn left through a slit in the wall and follow the river. The path for a while will appear to go into a wood, but returns to the riverside very soon. On reaching a stile with a yellow arrow, bear right up the steep open field, keeping to the right. At the top you will see Middleham Castle. Go downhill joining the lane back into town. Pass the castle to your left and head straight down through a cobbled alley, turning right at the bottom for the square.

# Romaldkirk Circular Walk

### ❧ Approximately 4 miles ❧

**Parking**

OS Map 92 Ref NY9922.
Romaldkirk village.

**Further Exploration**

**The Castle, Barnard Castle**
Built in 1125, the castle clings
to the steep banks of the Tees
and is now a ruin but still has a
12th-century keep and the
remains of a 14th-century hall.
Telephone 0833 38212

**Egglestone Abbey, Barnard Castle**
The remains of this
Premonstratensian abbey make
a picturesque sight on the right
bank of the River Tees. A large
part of the church can be seen,
as can the remains of monastic
buildings

The pub in the pretty village of Romaldkirk is the start and finish of this pleasant walk, which takes you through the beautiful, secluded and tree-lined gorge of the River Tees, past numerous rapids and waterfalls and back across open farmland.

## Rose and Crown (Free House)

Built in 1733, this very attractive stone-built hotel has a beamed bar whose cream walls are adorned with old farming tools and photographs of the village in the 1900s. There is a log fire, polished wooden chairs and tables, and lots of brass and copper which is also a feature of the wood-panelled Crown Room, where food is served. There is also a separate restaurant.

On draught: Theakston Best, Old Peculier, Younger Scotch, Carlsberg Hof, McEwans. Food: a varied menu is supplemented by daily specials; all dishes are home-cooked and typically may include courgette and pear soup (£1.65), langoustines with garlic mayonnaise (£3.95), Whitby scampi (£5.85), steak and mushroom pie cooked in Old Peculier (£5.95), and fresh pasta tossed in cream with peppers and mushrooms (£4.25). Puddings (£1.95) include hot apple and spiced brown Betty, fudgy nut pie, and shortbread and butterscotch tart; times are 12-1.30pm and 6.30-9.30pm.

Telephone 0833 50213.

L eaving the Rose and Crown Hotel, turn left to the church, then right across the road and village green, passing the Kirk Inn on your right. Straight in front there is a footpath sign; follow the track between two houses, then go straight on where the track bears left. The path continues for some distance between stone walls and hedges until you reach two gates. Take the left-hand gate and turn immediately left following the line of the stone wall. At the end of the stone wall, bear diagonally right across the field, heading for the large holly tree in the adjacent field. Go through the gate, and head diagonally left across this field to a large tree. Through a very narrow gate, walk down the gentle slope, past the farmhouse and cross the stone stile in the wall in front of you. Turn immediately left along the stone wall and at the end of this, turn right and follow a grass track down to the edge of the field. Go into the wood through the gate and follow the track straight on, gradually descending and keeping the river on your left. Soon you come to a stone stile, cross this and the stream and follow the path alongside the river, passing the rapids and waterfalls. (At one point the path takes you over mossy boulders where care must be taken). Eventually the path bears right and climbs up to a gate on the edge of the tree line. Having passed through the gate those who would like a more energetic walk can continue straight ahead towards the farm buildings. This path continues for several miles along the edge of the river. For the shorter walk, turn right diagonally across the field towards a stone barn. Go through the gate, past the barn on your right and head for the top right-hand corner of the field. Go through this gate and continue straight across the field to another gate and stile. Cross the field following the track to the stream, then after the stream, bear diagonally right to the gate with farm buildings in the distance. Through the gate, walk along the side of the hedge towards the stone wall and farm buildings. Cross the stile and then retrace your steps to the village and your car.

**Bowes Museum, Barnard Castle**
This splendid mansion, built in the style of a French chateau by John Bowes in 1869, houses an outstanding collection of works of art, including paintings, porcelain, silver, ceramics and tapestries.
Telephone 0833 690606

# Newton to Slaidburn

∾ Approximately 5 miles ∾

*A gently undulating outward route affording fine moorland and valley views, returning along the picturesque Hodder valley.*

**Parking**

OS Map 103 Ref SD6950. Newton village hall

Turn right, then immediately right again downhill passing the Parkers Arms to follow the road across the bridge over the River Hodder. Cross the stile on the left and follow the river bank. Carry straight on where the river bears left, through a metal gate and over a small concrete bridge. Turn right along a path through a group of trees before bearing left uphill across an open field. Through a gateway (no gate), turn right along a track and soon turn left along a lane. Turn right into the driveway of Manor House Farm, then left through a metal gate opposite the house. Beside a stream, bear left through an iron gate (yellow arrow) near the concrete bridge. Keep to the river's edge then, through another metal gate on the left, keep right and head for the barn which soon comes into view. Follow arrows through the farmyard, bearing left up the driveway to a lane. Cross this and the stile waymarked 'Slaidburn', and go uphill to pass through a metal gate, then head downhill beside a wall. Through a gate, carry straight on, to join a path down to a gate and the road. Turn left and walk down to Slaidburn and the pub.

# Hark to Bounty Inn
# (Scottish & Newcastle)

Dating back to the 13th century, the inn contains a remarkable courtroom on the first floor which was still in use as a court as recently as 1937 and had been used by travelling justices from the 14th century onwards, being the only courtroom between York and Lancaster. Now it is used as a function room, but retains the old jury benches and witness box. Downstairs the large open-plan bar has rustic wooden tables and chairs, polished brass and copperware, and an open fireplace. Outside, a riverside garden has a play area and barbecues are held in summer. Children are welcome.

On draught: Theakston Best and Old Peculier, Matthew Brown Mild, Guinness, McEwan, Beck's, Strongbow cider. Food: hearty bar snacks include home-made soup (£1.50), steak and kidney pie (£4.50), Forest of Bowland casserole (£5), ploughman's (£4), and sandwiches (from £2); times are 12-2pm and 6-9pm (restaurant 7-9pm). Other refreshment includes high tea(2-6pm), morning coffee and breakfasts (from 7.30am).

Telephone: 0200 446246.

**Further Exploration**
**Slaidburn Village**
The church dates back to 1246, the interior being graced by a shining three-decker pulpit and on display are the dog-whips wielded by the church wardens to keep the farmers' collies in order while their masters were at church. The vicar once had a dog called Bounty whose barking is immortalised in the name of the inn.

Retrace your steps through the village and then through the car park on the right to join a path beside the river. After two gates, cross a field heading towards the churchyard wall and through a gate beside a low shed. Head directly across the valley, through a kissing gate, bearing right then left onto an established track along the edge of the valley. Past Dunnow Hall, go straight on across the meadow through another kissing gate. Follow a track beside the river, bearing left through a gate and keep to the right-hand wall across the field. Cross a stile (waymarked) on the right and bear left across a small footbridge down to the river's edge. Follow the path through a gate to join the outward route by the road bridge and turn right for the return to the starting point.

# Dunsop Bridge to Whitewell

⮜ Approximately 4½ miles ⮞

*A gentle valley walk
alongside the River
Hodder with beautiful
views.*

**Parking**

OS Map 103 Ref SD6550

Car park at Dunsop Bridge

**Further exploration**

The Trough of Bowland is a wild
region of grouse moor and high
fells dissected by narrow, deep
valleys, once one of the ancient
royal forests of Saxon England.
This area of outstanding natural
beauty can be reached by a
lonely moorland road from
Dunsop Bridge.

From the car park, turn right along the road passing the post office, and cross the bridge over the River Dunsop. Bear left and walk along a farm driveway (waymarked), through a metal gate, and around the farm buildings before bearing right through iron gates onto a track beside a stone wall. Cross a stile into a large field and turn right onto a grassy path running parallel with the river. Remain on this meadowland path through two metal gates before bearing left uphill towards a farmhouse (Burholme). Go through a wooden gate onto a track, cross a small footbridge over a stream and then enter the farmyard. Follow the driveway away from the farm, eventually reaching a road beside a bridge. Bear left and follow the road to the pub.

The return walk simply retraces your steps back the way you came.

# Inn at Whitewell (Free House)

The inn stands next to the village church overlooking the River Hodder, in the most beautiful, unspoilt countryside. The main bar is old-fashioned, with antique settles, roundback chairs, a stone fireplace and heavy ceiling beams. An adjoining seating area includes the entrance hall where there are more settles and a piano usually covered with an array of daily papers and magazines. Many interesting prints and paintings adorn the walls and come from the inn's own art gallery. Along the corridors stuffed animals include a fox vanishing into the wall. There is a family room and a riverside garden with views across its three acres towards the Trough of Bowland.

On draught: Moorhouse's Pendle Witches Brew, Bentley's Yorkshire, Boddingtons, Chester's Best Mild, Murphy's, Guinness, Stella Artois, Heineken, Olde English cider. Food: bar meals are generously served and include dishes like chicken liver pâté (£4), Cumberland sausage (£5), fisherman's pie (£5.60), courgette lasagne (£4.80), salads (around £5), and sandwiches (from £2.50). Puddings (£2) are home-made, and there is an imposing selection of British cheese. Children's portions are available. The small restaurant serves an à la carte menu; times are 12-2pm and 7.15-9.30pm.

Telephone: 02008 222.

**Clitheroe Castle Museum, Clitheroe**
Nearby Clitheroe Castle has one of the smallest Norman keeps in England. The museum in Castle House includes displays on local history and the industrial archaelogy of the Ribble Valley. Special features include the restored Hacking ferry boat, a Victorian kitchen with taped commentary, and printer's and clogger's shops. Telephone: 0200 24635.

# Belle Grange to Near Sawrey

∽ Approximately 6½ miles ∽

*A pleasant walk through National Trust forest and across Claife Heights into Beatrix Potter country, with spectacular views of Windermere from the lake's quiet side.*

**Parking**

OS Map 97 Ref SD3899. Follow signs for the ferry to reach the car park.

**Further Exploration**

Hill Top, Near Sawrey (National Trust)

The little 17th-century house where Beatrix Potter wrote many of her books, is directly behind the Tower Bank Arms and contains the writer's furniture and china; her 'New Room', where she did much of her work, was restored in 1986. Telephone: 05394 36269.

Not far from Belle Grange is Hawkshead Grammar School which William Wordsworth attended as a pupil. It is open daily Mar to Oct.

Follow the path to Belle Grange House, and at the first house on your right, bear right and continue straight on through the forest, eventually following the signs for Sawrey. Pass between the two halves of Wise Een Tarn, on to Moss Eccles Tarn and into Near Sawrey. Bear left for the pub.

## Tower Bank Arms (Free House)

This small 17th-century country inn made an appearance in Beatrix Potter's tale of Jemima Puddleduck, and is now owned by the National Trust. The low-beamed bar is traditional; simply furnished with settles on the slate floor, and a big wood-burning stove. The walls are adorned with local hunting photographs, and the pub's labradors usually adorn the floor. There is a pleasant garden, and children are allowed in the eating area at lunchtime only. Service is always friendly and helpful, but the pub can get very crowded sometimes.

On draught: Theakston Best, XB, Old Peculier and Mild, Beck's and Dry Blackthorn cider. There is also a selection of reasonably priced wines, and even champagne. Food: bar meals include chicken breast filled with stilton and leeks (£6.75), cream cheese and broccoli pie (£4.25), filled rolls (from £2), ploughman's (£3.70) and, of course, sticky toffee pudding; times are 12-2pm and 6.30-9pm (from 7pm on Sundays).

Telephone: 05394 36334.

etrace your steps uphill to the turning for Far Sawrey. Follow the path to a metalled road, turn left and, immediately after the pub, left again up the track signposted to Claife Heights. At the next fork, bear right and pass through a gate. Follow the main path which eventually takes you through woods to the lake. Follow the lakeside path back to the car park.

**Beatrix Potter Gallery, Hawkshead (National Trust)**
Just a short distance from Near Sawrey, Hawkshead is home to the Beatrix Potter Gallery. This award-winning exhibition displays selected original drawings, and illustrations from her children's books. There is also a display of her life as an author, artist, farmer and active preserver of her beloved Lake District.
Telephone: 05394 36355.

# Threlkeld to Scales

~ Approximately 5 miles ~

*A low level walk along
pretty river banks and
the edges of the fells,
with good views of
northern Lakeland
peaks.*

**Parking**

OS Map 89 Ref NY3125.
Threlkeld car park just north of
the village on Blease road to
Blencathra.

**Further Exploration**

St. Mary's Church, Threlkeld
The present building is 18th-
century, but the original
foundation dates back to the
14th century and may be the
oldest chapelry in the diocese of
Carlisle.

L eave the car park on a public footpath to Threlkeld through a kissing gate. The path follows Blease Gill down to the village. At the road, turn right, and then left onto a public footpath along the side of St Mary's church. Cross a stile into a field which you then leave by a stile near the opposite corner. Cross the A66 and turn left to find another stile into a field on the right. Follow the path along the edge of the field, cross a stile by the River Glenderamackin and turn left to follow the path along the river bank. Cross a narrow footbridge over a small stream and continue along the main river bank. Cross over a minor road and follow the signpost to Guardhouse. The path continues for about a mile, crossing a metalled track to Keswick golf course, and a small stream. When the path turns left away from the river alongside a stream, cross a footbridge to reach a metalled track. Turn right and, just before Guardhouse bridge, you will see two public footpaths on your left. Take the path to Stone Raise which follows the river bank, then bears left along a fence. Continue to follow the fence as it bends sharply left, and cross the stile at the corner of the field. Bear right across the next field to pass to the left of a line of oak trees, heading in the direction of a whitewashed house. Leave this field by the stile ahead and the next field by a stile in the top right-hand corner. Follow the right edge of the next field to reach the A66. Turn right along the road and you will soon see the pub.

# White Horse Inn (Free House)

This whitewashed pub set into the hillside has no garden, but the profusion of flowers in the window boxes and in the strawberry pots standing between the benches outside, give a colourful patio effect. There is plenty of seating in the smart, spacious oak-beamed bar which also has an open fire and is decorated with pictures of hunting scenes and trophies. Children under five years old are not allowed inside in the evenings.

On draught: Jennings Bitter, Cumberland Ale, Marston's Pedigree, Guinness, Pilsner. There is also a range of malt whiskies. Food: the lunchtime menu includes peach halves with garlic cream cheese pâté and wholemeal bread, hot savoury flan of the day (both £3.95), ploughman's (£3.95) and Cumberland sausage with salad (£5.50). Sweets include sticky toffee ginger pudding and fudge ice cream (both £2.40). In the evenings the menu is more extensive and booking is advisable; times are 12-1.30pm and 7-8.30pm (in winter Fri and Sat evenings only).

Telephone: 07687 79241.

Turn right out of the pub and walk along the main road to reach a small house. Turn right up a farm track, go through a kissing gate in the stone wall ahead, and turn left onto the fells. Continue to follow the path along the fell foot, keeping the stone wall on your left. You will cross Scales Beck, pass Doddick Farm and then cross Doddick Gill. The path crosses a third stream (Gate Gill) and then continues through a gate in the same direction along the fell foot. After crossing two stiles, pass through a gate in front of Blease Gill and turn left before the stream to go through a second gate. Follow the path signposted to Threlkeld down the stream for the return to the car park.

# Crosthwaite to Strawberry Bank

~ Approximately 7 miles ~

*A fairly level walk
through pastoral
agricultural scenes and
lush ferned woodland
at Cartmel Fell.*

**Parking**
OS Map 97 Ref SD4491.
Crosthwaite church

From the car park, turn left and walk through the village, turning right at Starnthwaite to reach a signposted stile on the left. Cross this stile, bear left, and then right after the next stile. Join a paved lane and follow the arrows to a ladder stile, after which you walk down the left side of the field, turning left again at the corner. Walk on the right side of the next few fields, turning right at a bridleway, and left at a road. Turn right at the next junction and follow the next footpath on the left to Lamb Howe. At a house, turn left, following arrows into the woods, and then bear right at a fork. Reaching a road, turn right, then left at the bridleway. At an old barn, turn left then, at a road, turn right and left again onto another bridleway. Continue straight through the gates and on to Hollins Farm, up to the road, and you will see the pub on the right.

Head downhill from the pub, across a stone bridge and turn right. At a pylon on the left, cross the stone steps in the wall, then cross the fields to a road. Turn left, then right through a gate and cross several fields to join a track which runs through farm buildings and up to a road. Turn left and continue until you see a track on the right leading up to the escarpment. Go to the top, turn left, then turn left again at an opening in the wall, crossing a stile a few yards further on. Follow the field straight down to a farm track, turn right, left at the bridleway, and bear right at the next turning to join another road. At a sharp right turn, keep straight on, entering the field, and take the path towards the church, and into the car park.

## Masons Arms (Free House)

This is a lovely, remote, whitewashed pub with a large kitchen range, ancient country furniture and a tiny but astonishingly well stocked bar. Children are welcome until 9pm.

On draught: Thwaites, Younger No 3, and two home-brews, with around 200 bottled and canned brands ranging from Chinese Tsingtao to Venezuelan Polar Bear. Food: the menu includes such favourites as pâté and salad (£4.50) and Cajun chicken (£6.95); times are 12-2pm and 6-8.45pm.

Telephone: 05395 68486.

# Helton to Askham

&#8766; Approximately 5½ miles &#8766;

*An easy walk, ranging from wide open fells with spectacular mountain views, to cool riverside tracks through pleasant woodlands.*

**Parking**

OS Map 90 Ref NY5122. There is space near the postbox in Helton.

Climb west out of Helton village on a small paved road (no through road), crossing a cattle grid and heading out to Askham Fell. Stay on this road until you turn right onto the fell at a bridleway sign and follow the way to a crossroads sign. If you go on past the signpost for a few hundred yards you will see a spectacular view of Ullswater's first reach, but the route turns left at the signpost for Askham on another bridleway. You will shortly see a line of trees directly ahead at the top of the incline, while a less pronounced track bears right towards a larger wood. Take this track which, after another mile, goes through a gate and joins a paved road into Askham. At the crossroads, take the road to the right of the general store, and you will soon see the pub on your right.

# Punch Bowl Inn(Whitbread)

This is a handsome inn with a large open bar, wooden beams and inglenooks, decorated with brasses and a variety of 'country life' implements and ornaments. Furnished with plain wooden tables, chairs and settles, it is a friendly and lively place to visit, with a thriving local clientele. Children are welcome.

On draught: Castle Eden Ale, Murphy's, Guinness, Stella Artois, Woodpecker and Strongbow ciders. There is also an interesting wine list which includes a few ports. Food: the menu offers a wide choice, from snacks like deep-fried mushrooms (£2.70) and fried stilton (£3.35) to turkey bake (£4.95) and large portions of spare ribs (£5.85), for example. Vegetarians do well, and there is a children's menu. Sweets (around £2.50) may include toffee cheesecake and fresh orange meringue pie; times are 12-2pm and 6.30-9.30pm (7-9pm in winter).

Telephone: 0931 712443.

**Further Exploration**

Lowther Castle

This early 19th-century building was the work of Sir Robert Smirke, architect of Covent Garden Theatre and the British Museum. It is now just a façade, having been gutted to reduce maintenance costs. The chapel vault and nave survive, parts parts dating from 1170. Some of the stone columns are carved with grotesque beasts.

O n leaving the pub, turn right, past the church and over the bridge. If you want to take a look at Lowther Castle, continue on this road to the chapel, then follow the footpath opposite. Return to the bridge to continue the walk. From the direction of the pub, turn right directly after the bridge along the footpath which follows the river. Stay on this riverside walk for about two miles, passing through woods, out onto open land and eventually entering another wood at Whale. Keeping on the right-hand side of the wood, you will emerge at a stile. Cross the corner of the field towards another stile behind a farmhouse. Cross this and walk beside the farmhouse, crossing another stile onto a road. Turn right, follow the road to a T-junction and go straight ahead onto a bridleway, heading for the river. Cross a footbridge, then follow the bridleway, eventually crossing a road into Helton. Walk straight on up a short track to another road, turn right through the village, then left to your car.

# Ireton Pike to Nether Wasdale

~ Approximately 5 miles ~

*Rugged scenery in a relatively little visited part of the Lake District characterises an exhilarating walk with fine views of Wastwater*

**Parking**

OS Map 89. Ref NY1201. Ireton Pike picnic area.

**Further exploration**

Biggest and Best

At the head of the three-mile-long stretch of Wastwater is the parish of Wasdale Head, where England's highest mountain - Scafell Pike - rises to 3,206ft - her deepest lake - Wastwater - measures 250ft deep, her smallest church - St Olaf's - has the smallest cubic capacity of any still in use, being only 35ft 9in by 14ft 2in with walls 6ft 6in high. Finally, in the 19th century, the landlord of a local hotel, Will Ritson, who had the knack of telling a good story, was dubbed the 'World's Biggest Liar'.

From the car park turn right along the lane and shortly take the footpath on the right signed Wasdale. Follow the path uphill through woodland, keeping right where the path forks, then at the top of the hill pass through a gate to leave the wood. Proceed along a well worn path across open moorland with spectacular views left into the River Irt valley. When the path peters out, maintain your direction with a wall to your right. After three-quarters of a mile at a crossroads of paths turn left and head steeply downhill. Nether Wasdale and Wastwater can be seen ahead, with the large chimneys of Sellafield Nuclear Plant away to your left. The defined path passes through a double gate, between two fences and over a few bridges as you walk through a sparse wood. At the end of the wood a waymarker points the way towards Nether Wasdale with an impressive view of Wastwater and the scree slopes. Follow the well worn path across fields and to the left of Flass House to a road. Turn right, cross a bridge and bear left into the village for the Screes Hotel.

## The Screes Hotel (Free House)

This is a traditional white-painted Cumbrian inn with exposed beams, open fires, comfortable seating and a welcoming country atmosphere in the two cosy bars The inn has five bedrooms for guests and children are welcome.

On draught: Theakston Best Bitter and Old Peculier, Yates Bitter, a guest ale, Beck's, Carlsberg, and Strongbow cider. There is also a large (over 50) selection of malt whiskies. Food: the popular bar menu features steak and kidney pie (£4.50), sirloin steak (£8), Cumberland sausages (£4.25), sandwiches (from £1.25), soup (£1.35) and vegetarian dishes like nut roast with a tangy tomato and garlic sauce (£4.50); times are 12-2pm and 6.30-9pm.

Telephone: 09467 26262.

From the inn, walk along the road, pass the Strands Hotel, then follow the waymarked path signed Gaterigg. Pass through a gate, bear left to a kissing gate, then follow the well defined path across a field to another gate and walk along the edge of the wood. Go through a gate and cross a stone bridge to walk up round the edge of Stangends Farm (NT). Turn left through the farmyard, then follow the farm track down to the road. Cross over, climb a stile and bear right through a gate, then head diagonally across the field to the foot of the hill. Cross a stile in the top right-hand corner of the field and follow the path through rhododrendrons and woodland to a stile. Cross it, bear right onto a well worn track and continue through dense woodland, shortly to bear left through a gate into a deciduous wood. On reaching a farm and a fork in the path, bear right and descend behind the farm to a farm track. Turn left and follow the track to a road. Turn left again and remain on the road for three-quarters of a mile back to your car.

# Baybridge to Blanchland
~ Approximately 5 miles ~

*A pleasant walk through farmland and along the Derwent river. Watch out for pied and grey wagtails and curlews.*

**Parking**

OS Map 87 Ref NY9549. Baybridge car park and picnic area

**Further Exploration**

Blanchland

This small, isolated village is thought to be named after the white habits of the Premonstratensian monks who settled there in the 12th century. The present church was built in 1752 using those parts of the old abbey church which had survived. There are three fine medieval tombstones on the transept floor, and many interesting artefacts.

**L**eave the picnic area and cross the road to find a track along the left bank of the river, signposted to Blanchland. Continue on this path, crossing several stiles on the way, to Blanchland, where the path leads to the left of the bridge, across the road and immediately right behind the wall of the bridge to reach the river bank again. Follow the river past three buildings on your left, the last being a derelict barn. Here the path becomes a track which you follow between two stone walls away from the river. At the top, this bears round to the left to reach a metalled road. Follow the road to the left back to Blanchland, turn left and the pub is on your left.

## Lord Crewe Arms (Free House)

Originally an abbot's dwelling for the nearby abbey, part of the cloisters can still be seen in the inn's terraced gardens. There are huge fireplaces in the bars, with one of the 13th-century inglenooks containing a priest hole. One of the bars is down in a crypt which has a stone-flagged arched roof, and is furnished with pews. The main bar has fine beams, old settles, and numerous photographs adorn the walls. The inn is named after an eighteenth-century aristocrat Lord Crewe, Bishop of Durham, who owned the village and, on his death, left it to a trust to ensure that it remained unaltered. Children are welcome in the restaurant.

On draught: Vaux Samson, Carlsberg, Lorimers, Guinness. Food: typical dishes are soup (£1.70), filled granary rolls (from £2.30) and grilled pork and apple burgers with chips and salad (£4.95); times are 12-2pm and 7-9pm (9.30 at weekends).

Telephone: (0434) 675251.

Turn right out of the pub and take the second track on your right just before you reach the car park. Bear left between two stone walls and follow the track up into the woods, keeping the stone shed on your right. The path meets a grass track which you follow to the left until you reach an iron gate. Through this gate, turn left across the field to reach another gate leading to a metalled road, with cottages on your right. Turn right along the road until you see a gate and a track on the right which leads back from the road. Follow the track through the gate to an iron gate in a stone wall. Pass through the gate and strike diagonally left to climb onto Penny Pie Fell, bearing north-west. As you reach the top, you will see a black barn ahead. Keep the wall on your left and cross a small stream to pass to the left of the barn. The track continues straight through an iron gate in a stone wall, then through another immediately on your right. From here, head diagonally left over the crest of the hill to reach another iron gate in a wall, and yet another at the lower right-hand corner. The track descends to the left to reach Penny Pie House, and your route follows it away to the right of the farm after crossing a stream. With the wall on your left, continue along the track which eventually becomes a metalled road, passing through a wooded area. There are two more iron gates to pass through before reaching the road at Baybridge. Turn right here and return to the picnic area.

# Howdiemont Sands to Craster

~ Approximately 6 miles ~

*A walk of contrasting scenery - woodland on the way out, spectacular coastal path on the return.*

**Parking**
OS Map 81 Ref NU2615
Howdiemont Sands

**Further Exploration**
The beaches along the early part of the walk, with their combination of miles of golden sand and extensive rock flats reaching out into the sea are beautiful, and relatively quiet due to their isolation.

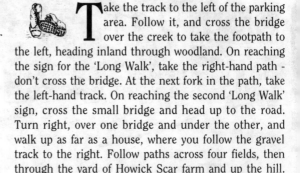

Take the track to the left of the parking area. Follow it, and cross the bridge over the creek to take the footpath to the left, heading inland through woodland. On reaching the sign for the 'Long Walk', take the right-hand path - don't cross the bridge. At the next fork in the path, take the left-hand track. On reaching the second 'Long Walk' sign, cross the small bridge and head up to the road. Turn right, over one bridge and under the other, and walk up as far as a house, where you follow the gravel track to the right. Follow paths across four fields, then through the yard of Howick Scar farm and up the hill. Follow the track down to a road which leads to the pub which you will find on the right.

## Jolly Fisherman (Vaux)

This traditional fishermen's pub has cosy bars, low ceilings, beams, brasses and seascapes on the walls, with lovely views of the sea and rocky beach. There is an open fire in the lounge bar.

On draught: Lorimers Best Scotch and Samson, Beamish, Labatts, Carlsberg Export, Wards, Guinness, plus Woodpecker and Strongbow cider. Food: the short menu features various burgers (£1), stottie cake pizzas (£1), Bockaneer - a large German sausage in a baguette (£1.50) - and sandwiches (from £1); times are 11am-3pm and 6-11pm. Telephone: 0665 576218.

Turn left from the pub car park down to the shore path, heading back towards Howdiemont Sands. The coastal path is waymarked, so continue to the signposts indicating coastal and inland paths. Take the inland path, following the route as waymarked to the creek and bridge of the outward route, cross the bridge and follow the track back to the car park.